PATAGONIA

• HISTORY, MYTHS AND LEGENDS •

revised edition

ROBERTO HOSNE

PATAGONIA
• HISTORY, MYTHS AND LEGENDS •
revised edition

Translated by
Carol Duggan

CONTENTS

PATAGONIA

FOREWORD

The object of this book is to offer the reader a perspective of Patagonia starting from the discovery of the Estrecho de Magallanes and continuing until modern times.

Throughout the history of this region there have always been dreams and illusions urging the conquerors and colonists to explore these lands, to possess them and settle down. We think this utopia must have been necessary to counteract the hardships and tremendous sacrifices demanded by the rough environment of Patagonia with its desolate lands and implacable weather.

Darwin referred to it as «a cursed land», and the seaman Antonio de Córdoba described it as «the most wretched and unfortunate part of the earth».

On the other hand, the explorer Ramón Lista was fascinated by Patagonia. He said: «Everything here stirs our deepest emotions: sometimes it is the sad barrenness of the plains; or the magnificent chaos of its mountains...»

What we can say, without any doubt, is that nobody has shown indifference towards this territory.

The natives, who were the original inhabitants of this region, suffered persecution and were subject to what could be described as a war of extermination. And yet, personalities like George Ch. Musters, Francisco P. Moreno or the eccentric Popper, among others, wrote very acute and positive observations about the Indians, their customs, the characteristics of different tribes and their attitudes, showing a deep insight into their idiosyncrasy.

The history of Patagonia is the history of a great adventure that began with the expeditions of famous navigators, pirates, and fierce *conquistadores* and continued afterwards with the brave, persevering explorers, the silent heroism of the settlers, the bloody combats between the white men and the Indians. Unlike other regions of Argentina, there are few characters in its history, but they stand out due to the fact that they came from different parts of the world, and they had to face the most extreme circumstances, all of which resulted in fascinating experiences.

Patagonia is like a huge scenario with an unending display of unusual episodes and a rich variety of characters: unscrupulous adventurers, devoted settlers, international fugitives –such as the gunmen from the North American Far West- immigrants like the Welsh or the Bóers, anxious to live in a place that would show tolerance and respect for their beliefs and traditions, communities that were willing to make a sacrifice because they believed in a future of welfare and prosperity.

This enigmatic territory made of desert and rock, of lakes and mountains, of glaciers and rivers of turbulent waters, of very high and very low temperatures, and the ever-present wind, all this suggests a land of violent beauty.

During almost five hundred years this vast territory has attracted all kinds of people, each pursuing his own particular dream, all willing to pay the price to keep the fire of their illusions burning.

This is a history made of strong passions: greed, lust for gold or power, the ambition to discover and to conquer, the will to overcome difficulties, the challenge behind scientific quests, the courage to explore and face unknown circumstances, the daily act of faith when a man´s life and values are at stake.

Roberto Hosne

1.- THE DISCOVERY

Magallanes and his remarkable feat – Mutiny and executions – Tragedy begins – A succession of different expeditions – First contact with the natives – Trapalanda, origin of the myth

Patagonia: a word that transports the reader to a magic, fascinating territory. As vast as it is unknown, it is conjured up in our imagination in many different ways.

It has always been a land of conquest and colonization, ever since Fernando de Magallanes discovered the Patagonian coast and the Strait that bears his name.

These desolate shores were host to famous navigators who suffered the savage force of its characteristic, unceasing wind. That, plus the doubtful hospitality of barren lands where nothing grows and no water can be found. Getting there was a notable feat. But settling down was practically impossible.

Magallanes discovered these lands by chance. His aim was to reach the "Islas de la Especiería" (Molucas) and return to Spain with his vessels laden with spices, silk, porcelain and all sorts of valuable goods he could find on the way. Like Columbus, he believed it was possible to get to the East through the West. And this trip was supposed to be the proof of his hypothesis.

The expedition consisted of five ships, (*San Antonio, Trinidad, Concepción, Victoria* and *Santiago*) Magallanes commanding this enterprise. Although each ship had its own captain, it was he who had the responsibility of the final decisions. In fact, shortly after leaving port he decided to change the pre-established route, and, coasting Africa up to Guinea, gave orders to veer towards Brazil. Juan de Cartagena, general overseer and captain of the *San Antonio,* demanded an explanation. Magallanes, who was obviously not used to answering for his decisions, considered this as a sort of insult and promptly relieved Juan de Cartagena of his duties as overseer replacing him with Antonio de Coca (accountant of the expedition). After this incident Magallanes became rather paranoid and, suspicious of his captains' intentions, he finally replaced Antonio de Coca by a cousin, Alvaro de Mezquita. The voyage continued with these conflicts until they reached Brazil. They stayed there for two weeks in the company of friendly natives, and maybe this relaxing fortnight helped to ease the tension.

Nevertheless, after a month and a half sailing, Magallanes realized that the calculations of the map he was using (drawn by Martín Behaim) were wrong. He kept this secret from the other captains and refused to follow their suggestions to find a secure port where they could take shelter, get supplies and maintenance for the ships. Magallanes, very self-assured, managed to impose his authority. On the 31ˢᵗ of March 1520 they reached a bay which he named Bahía San Julián, where they disembarked in order to spend the winter. Food and wine were rationed and the men were both discouraged and resentful.

The captains considered it was the perfect moment to encourage mutiny, and that marked the beginning of an episode where treachery, cruelty and murder haunted the days and nights of these tough, fierce sailors.

The leaders of the insurrection were Quesada, Mendoza and Cartagena who, together with a group of men, boarded the *San Antonio*. They took Alvaro de Mezquita prisoner, and stabbed Juan Elgorriaga because he confronted them, thus making it quite clear that from that moment they gave the orders. Juan Sebastián Elcano was appointed captain.

Next morning one of the ships, the *Trinidad*, sent a boat with some of the crew to the mutineer ship to ask for someone to accompany them to land in search of wood and water. But nobody moved, and a voice informed them that they took orders only from Gaspar de Quesada. The men returned to inform Magallanes about the situation. On the other hand the mutineers, scared because of the possible –and very severe- consequences of their rebellion, asked to be received by the admiral to begin conversations.

Magallanes took the messengers prisoner and, in turn, sent a boat with Gonzalo Gómez de Espinosa with a written reply. Luis Mendoza, captain of the *Victoria*, received Espinosa who in cold blood stuck a dagger right in the captain´s throat while he was reading the note. The crew looked on, paralyzed with shock, and that was when another fifteen armed men sent by Magallanes took command of the ship, and named Duarte de Barbosa (Magallanes´s father-in-law) captain of the *Victoria*. He led this ship alongside the *Trinidad*, which was controlling the entry to the bay.

Mendoza and Quesada were tried and sentenced to death. Both were beheaded and their bodies, ripped to pieces, were stuck on poles, displayed for everyone to see.

Such was the way treachery was punished in those days.

There were other men killed, and presumably some were pardoned because their work on board was necessary, but pardon was shown as an act of mercy.

Magallanes had to face another problem, he had to soften the terrible impact of these dramatic events and keep his crew busy and active. He decided to build a workshop with a forge and have everybody´s attention focused on repairing the ships.

Two months went by before they made their first contact with the natives. These were described as being *"big as giants, very well built, their wide faces dyed red except for the eyes which were surrounded by yellow circles, and two heart-shaped traces on their cheeks"*.

Magallanes was believed to have called these natives Patagones on account of their enormous feet.

The natives were quite friendly at first, but the newcomers –in a style which was typical of the *conquistadores*- thought they could take some of them back to Spain in bondage. As they couldn´t take them on board by force, they thought of a way to trick them. They showed the natives some iron chains to attract their attention, and then, pretending it was a present, they put the chains round their ankles. When the natives realized they were prisoners they got furious and started to fight. A sailor was wounded with a poisoned arrow and died instantly. The Spaniards retaliated with firearms but the natives managed to get away. Not only were they very fast runners, they also ran in a sort of zigzag so in the end they fooled their would-be captors, who, spitefully, burnt down their huts.

One month later Magallanes decided it was time to leave this region although his mission was far from completed.

In October a fearful storm pushed the ships southward until they reached a headland which they christened Cabo de las Once Mil Vírgenes. Further on, seeing what looked like an estuary, Magallanes sent the *Concepción* and *San Antonio* to explore. They had five days to carry out this reconnaissance, and meanwhile the remaining ships waited nearby, in a place called "Bahía de la Posesión".

A few days went by and suddenly the ships were seen coming back, cannons saluting, flags waving, sailors enthusiastically jumping, embracing one another… Victory was theirs!

The passage to the Pacific had finally been discovered.
Magallanes had triumphed.

In those hard days, celebrations didn´t last long.
Future actions must be decided, new decisions must be taken. Due to the lack of supplies, the weariness of the crew and the bad condition of the ships, the general opinion among the captains favored returning to Spain.

But Magallanes refused and gave orders to sail towards the Molucas, his original destination.

He met his death on the island of Mactan, fighting with the natives, on the 27th of April 1521. He was forty-one.

The itinerary was continued by Elcano, who reached Spain on board the *Victoria*, on the 8th of September 1522, thus completing the first circumnavigation of the globe as had been planned by Magallanes.

This was undoubtedly the biggest nautical feat of the times.

The conquest

The time of discovery was also the time of cruelty, of savage ambitions, of unlimited power.

Magallanes´s voyage defined a certain style which would be imitated by other conquerors.

His expedition was the first to make contact with natives of that region. They seemed friendly at first, but in the end they turned against the conquerors who were cruel and domineering from the very beginning.

His fierce determination was perhaps the cause of his success, but his authoritative ways finally drove his captains to mutiny; they met their death at the gallows that Magallanes had specially built for this occasion.

Sixty years later Francis Drake made use of this particular scenario to execute another rebel, Thomas Doughty.

Subsequent expeditions were not very successful, they faced all the logical drawbacks of long voyages in distant, hostile lands.

Five years after Magallanes discovered the Strait another expedition was sent by Spain. This time García Jofre de Loaisa was in command. Sailing master was Juan Sebastián Elcano. This expedition had a tragic end. Some of the ships were wrecked, others were boarded by pirates; the fact is that none of the ships returned to Spain. Loaisa and Elcano both died on the voyage.

It was only in 1537 –twelve years later- that the only survivor, Andrés de Urdaneta, was able to return to his country. He presented the Spanish Court with a full report of Loaisa´s tragic expedition; fearing all this information could discourage future expeditions, the authorities decided to keep the report secret.

The third expedition left under the command of Simón de Alcazaba, a deft navigator and also an expert in cosmography. The expedition consisted of two rather old ships (the *Madre de Dios* and the *San Pedro*) and a crew of two hundred and fifty men with doubtful reputations.

First they attempted crossing the Estrecho de Magallanes (Magellan Straits), but they were violently stopped by a terrible storm, ice-cold rain and a lashing wind that could easily wreck the ships. They also found the remains of the shipwrecked *Sancti Spiritu* –débris of Loaisa´s expedition- which the crew took as an ill omen so, in spite of Alcazaba´s determination to proceed, he was finally convinced to try and cover the distance by land.

They landed at a place they called Puerto Leones (Chubut) and tried to reach Chile by land. But the lack of fresh water, sickness and exhaustion forced some of them to return to Puerto Leones. The others went on their way and had a friendly encounter with the *Tehuelche* Indians who provided them with food and water. But, to their disappointment, there was no gold or silver or precious stones to be found. Considering that most of these men had accepted to go on this voyage with vague promises of all sorts of riches and goods, this disappointment may have produced a desire for vengeance. At least fifty men had already died and the rest were either sick or exhausted. Maybe it was the feeling of having been deceived that drove them to mutiny. In this state of mind they decided to return to Puerto Leones. Captains Juan Arias and Gaspar Sotelo, together with a group of soldiers, rebelled. They took Rodrigo de Isla and Juan Mori prisoner. Arias wanted to kill them so he could dedicate his efforts to something more lucrative such as piracy. But this was not a unanimous opinion. Some were afraid of making matters worse by killing the head men, so they went their way. But Sotelo was intent on killing Alcazaba, which is precisely what he did the night they secretly returned to Puerto Leones. Alcazaba was stabbed during his sleep. And so were other men who had remained loyal to him. The dead bodies were thrown into the sea.

As usual in these situations, when authority has been overturned, it is difficult to maintain discipline. In a group formed by killers and their accomplices it is hard to establish ranks. Who is entitled to give orders and on what grounds can they expect obedience?

In the midst of this confusion, Juan Mori with a group of men loyal to him recovered the authority of which he had been deprived.

Arias and Sotelo were tried and beheaded, Gallego and Halcón were hanged, and another four mutineers with stones round their necks were thrown into the sea to feed the fish.

Once order was re-established the ships went back to sea, leaving behind the remaining rebels and also the sick, who would most likely have been unable to outlive another hard winter.

In August of 1539 a fleet of three vessels left Sevilla; only one managed to cross the Estrecho de Magallanes and reach the coast of Peru; another returned to Spain after exploring the Canal de Beagle, and the third was shipwrecked before crossing the Strait, although the hundred and fifty members of the crew were presumably able to land; seventeen years later, only two survivors, Antonio de Cobos and Pedro de Oviedo, actually reached Concepción, in Chile. They told of the most fascinating adventures in a beautiful city called Trapalanda. This city was placed next to an equally beautiful lake, and surrounded by a fabulous landscape. It was also supposed to be full of treasures and precious metals but was never seen by anybody else. These stories were the origin of the legend which excited the imagination of adventure-lovers and the greed of those bold fortune-hunters who dedicated their lives to the pursuit of personal dreams of gold, silver and power.

This was not the only myth about those lands that existed at the time. Another, equally fantastic, described the incredible Ciudad de los Césares.

A possible explanation is that in those days success was infrequent. Expeditions and voyages usually met a tragic end. Failure in the quest for gold, riches, power, etc. could not be accepted, and therefore the myths and all these fabulous stories appeared, exciting the imagination, awakening, once again, fantastic dreams and impossible ambitions which disguised the disappointment that reality had to offer.

2.- PIRATES AHOY!

Francis Drake appears on the scene – The misfortunes of Sarmiento de Gamboa - Enter Cavendish, feared pirate and expert navigator – Spaniards are worried due to the presence of English, Dutch and French ships in the South Seas – Dutch sailors discover a new gateway to the Pacific – In search of the enchanted "Ciudad de los Césares"- Narborough´s attempt to settle a base in Deseado

Years later, in December 1577, the fearful Francis Drake left the port of Plymouth commanding five ships, on a secret mission of boarding Spanish ships as they left Peru laden with precious metals. This, in spite of the good relationship between England and Spain at the time.

After five months at sea they reached the place that Drake called Bahía de las Focas, which could be at present Puerto Deseado; the following month they got to San Julián. Drake had the gallows repaired (originally built by Magallanes) and ordered the execution of Thomas Doughty, accused of mutiny. Later accounts of his death state that he was given the choice of returning to England to be tried, or to be left on his own in these foreign lands, or to be beheaded. Being a gentleman, Thomas Doughty chose the last. Records say that he took Holy Communion, embraced Drake, took leave of the crew and then prayed for the Kingdom and Her Majesty. Finally, he bent his head and offered it to his executioner.

On the 20th of August 1578 Drake's fleet entered the Estrecho de Magallanes and covered the distance in only sixteen days which was, in those days, quite a record. During the crossing Drake changed the name of his ship *Pelikan* to *Golden Hind*.

The Pacific Ocean welcomed Drake´s expedition with a tremendous storm. As a result, the *Elizabeth* was deviated from its course and returned to Spain while the *Marygold* capsized. Drake´s ship was adrift for almost two months, but thanks to that he was able to discover the latitude where the waters from both oceans mix. This was later confirmed by the Dutch when they discovered Cabo the Hornos (Cape Horn).

Drake then sailed north up to California. On the way he boarded ships and ransacked villages. Loot and pillage were the main activity of this lord of the sea who became one of the most feared pirates in history.

He was able to combine discovery with good fortune: he decided to return to England and when his ship, the *Golden Hind*, was so laden with valuable goods that it could hold no more he returned via the Molucas and the Cabo de Buena Esperanza, thus describing the second circumnavigation of the globe.

Unlike most of the adventurers of the sea, Drake made such large profits for the Crown that he was knighted; some time later he married a very rich girl and became a member of Parliament.

It is believed that these most valuable cargoes brought to the English Crown by their famous pirates were the basis of England's financial power.

Sarmiento de Gamboa

Faced with the danger of pirates -and most specially Francis Drake- the Viceroy of Peru appointed Pedro Sarmiento de Gamboa for the defense of all ships and settlements on the Pacific coast.

Sarmiento de Gamboa was probably chosen because he was a very deft sailor, a brave *conquistador* and also a cartographer. He was also very keen on astrology, which caused him no end of trouble with the Inquisition. Persecution, torture and finally a firm decision to condemn him to exile. That was when Francisco de Toledo, Viceroy of Peru, intervened and assigned him the mission of designing a defensive plan.

Therefore, Gamboa carried out a reconnaissance of the Estrecho de Magallanes, looking for appropriate sites to establish settlements and strategic defenses. He returned to Spain explaining to the King the basis of his project and, with the King's approval, organized an expedition consisting of twenty-three ships and around three thousand people including sailors, soldiers, settlers, thirty women and twenty-three children. Diego Flores de Valdez was appointed chief of the expedition, Alonso de Sotomayor Governor of Chile, and Sarmiento de Gamboa Governor of the Estrecho. This was the largest and most important expedition ever sent to the extreme south of Patagonia.

Due to the insistence of Diego de Valdez, and against the better judgement of Sarmiento de Gamboa who knew there were storms ahead and it was advisable to postpone the trip, the expedition finally left port on the 25th of September 1581. A few days later, Sarmiento de Gamboa´s hunch proved to be true, disaster causing the disappearance of four ships and eight hundred people. That decided them to cast anchor at Cádiz, remaining there for a month. They finally left with sixteen ships, but that expedition was already doomed. During the voyage a plague caused fifty-one deaths, and then, when in Rio de Janeiro, another two hundred men died. Going south, towards Patagonia, they lost another ship and three hundred more people died. An encounter with Edward Fenton, the pirate, meant the loss of another ship. This series of disasters produced serious disagreements between the leaders of the expedition, and a slackening of discipline. The nine ships that sailed towards the Rio de la Plata were later reduced to eight, and when they finally reached Buenos Aires, the three visible heads of the expedition decided to part company. Alonso de Sotomayor went to Chile by land, convinced that it was safer than travelling by sea. Flores de Valdez decided to return to Spain. And Sarmiento de Gamboa remained in command of the expedition.

On the 1st of February 1584 Sarmiento de Gamboa reached the Estrecho with five ships and five hundred and thirty-eight crew-men. He founded Ciudad de Nombre de Jesús next to Cabo Vírgenes, a place of winds, cold and permanent storms. He traced the city plan and distributed plots of land where a few shacks were built, plus a church and a primitive City Hall. But the people were dissatisfied. Lack of adequate clothing, insufficient food and a hostile climate were the cause of Captain Diego de la Ribera´s decision to return to Spain with his ship, and three other ships followed suit. That left Sarmiento de Gamboa with only one ship, the *Santa María de Castro*, and three hundred and eight people. The prospect of settling in such an unsuitable place urged Sarmiento de Gamboa to search for something more appropriate and he finally founded another city in Punta Santa Ana, about four hundred kilometers away from Nombre de Jesús. He sailed with fifty crew-men and one hundred settlers went on foot. It took them fifteen days to reach their new home, having ample opportunity to test the belligerence of the Indian tribes of that region.

Sarmiento de Gamboa called the new town Ciudad del Rey Felipe: they built a small fort, a church and wooden huts, all surrounded by a fence. But it turned out to be a barren land. When the people began to feel hungry there was a general state of discontent that ended in mutiny. Sarmiento de Gamboa hanged the rebels and, in control of the situation, decided to go back to Nombre de Jesús in search of food. His idea was to cast anchor in Cabo Vírgenes. He never managed to get to the Estrecho on account of the storm that pushed him up north to Rio de Janeiro. In despair he begged the authorities in Spain to send help to those who remained waiting in the Estrecho; but that help never came.

In June 1586 he decided to return to Spain, but his ship was boarded by Walter Raleigh who took him prisoner to England. In spite of being a prisoner he was well treated. He was received by Queen Elizabeth who set him free and used him as a courier with a message to Felipe II. When travelling through France he was taken prisoner and tortured. Four years later, once the ransom was paid he was again set free. But by that time, when he finally reached Spain, Sarmiento de Gamboa was a sick old man. He wrote to the king begging for help for the people who remained in the Estrecho whom he considered were still alive and waiting. But he received no answer.

Actually, at the time there were still a few survivors in Rey Felipe: three women and fifteen men, who decided to march towards Nombre de Jesús on the slim chance of finding some help.

One day in January of 1587, these few survivors, who had already reached Bahía Posesión, saw some sails in the distance. It was the fleet of Thomas Cavendish, the English pirate who had left Plymouth in 1536 with three ships. He traveled all along the Patagonian coast and anchored in the same place that Drake had chosen -called by him Bahía de las Focas-. Cavendish gave the place a new name, that of his own ship, "Desire" (which later became "Deseado").

When they entered the Estrecho they saw the survivors in Bahía Posesión. One of the Spaniards managed to board the ship and the others were waiting to follow suit. Suddenly they saw the ship leaving and abandoning them to their own fate. With surprise and despair they watched their last chance of salvation sailing away.

What could have been the reason for such a cruel attitude?

A possible explanation was afforded by later reports which referred to the sudden appearance of favorable winds; those, being so scarce, decided Cavendish to grasp the opportunity and continue with the voyage even if it meant leaving seventeen helpless people behind. Tomás Hernández, the only

Spaniard who was rescued, later told this tragic story.

When Cavendish sailed by Rey Felipe he decided to anchor. He couldn´t have seen a more pathetic picture. In his chronicles, master Francis Perry told that "the Spaniards had hanged some of their companions", and as to the others:

> *"They died like dogs in their homes, fully dressed, and that is how we found them when we arrived, until the village reeked of the stench of dead bodies".*

The unfortunate inhabitants had apparently dragged themselves to their beds with their last breath and awaited death.

The English took their supply of water and firewood and all the weapons and cannons they could find. Then they burnt the village down. They christened the place with the appropriate name of "Port Famine"

On the 1st of January 1590, the only survivor of Sarmiento de Gamboa's expedition was rescued by the *Delight of Bristol* whose captain was the English pirate Andrew Merrick. But he never reached England, he died on the voyage.

The lust for gold

The Estrecho de Magallanes was the gateway to all the important gold and silver centers in Peru. It attracted pirates from all over the world. The English had become experts at looting and were already a menace to the Spaniards, but the Dutch weren't far behind.

In June 1598 a Dutch fleet under the orders of Jacobo Mahu traveled towards the Estrecho, but scurvy, hunger and fighting against the English and the Spaniards gradually maimed its forces. Crossing the Strait took them four months and cost many lives due to the cold, diseases and people who just froze to death or disappeared in a blizzard. The ships separated, one was seized by the Spaniards and the other, called *Geelof*, returned to Holland.

In September 1598 Oliver Van Noort left Amsterdam commanding four vessels. A year later they reached Deseado. Van Noort crossed the Estrecho right into the Pacific Ocean and traveled along its coasts looting and boarding other ships with a ferocity worthy of Francis Drake.

In 1615 the expedition of the Compañía Austral launched two ships, the

Hoorn and *Concordia* under Guillermo Schouten's command. Their first stop was Deseado, where the *Hoorn* burnt down. Continuing the voyage with the only ship left they traveled around Tierra del Fuego and the island they named Isla de los Estados. They got a glimpse of the Sebaldines (now Malvinas), and discovered the strait they called Le Maire which was later changed to Cap Hoorn (Cabo de Hornos) in honor of the ship that was burnt down.

This new crossing into the Pacific discovered by the Dutch (Le Maire and Cap Hoorn) made the Spaniards very uneasy. Up to that moment the only access to the Pacific Ocean had been through the Estrecho de Magallanes, which was under their control. But now they had to face a different situation. Therefore, Spain sent two expert navigators, Bartolomé and Gonzalo de Nodal, to corroborate this information. Carrying out their task entailed sailing all around Tierra del Fuego, passing through the Estrecho Le Maire, reaching Cape Hoorn and returning -via the Estrecho de Magallanes to the Atlantic Ocean- to Spain. Not only did they prove the Dutch discoveries to be true, they also provided very valuable maps for future voyages and research.

But all this strengthened the idea of a menace to Spain´s exclusive power in that part of the world.

The next expedition, in 1670, was also sent by the English Crown; Captain John Narborough, in command of two ships, sailed to the Patagonian coasts on a study and reconnaissance voyage, specially concerning habits and characteristics of the Indian natives. A storm separated both ships, and while Narborough waited for the *Batchelor Pink* at a pre-arranged meeting point, he made good use of his time and explored all that region; in a strange improvised ceremony he hoisted the British flag, ordered the cannons to shoot and formally declared that place to be called Port Desire, of exclusive English property. Actually, they waited in vain for the *Batchelor Pink* to arrive with all the building materials it carried, because it had deserted.

In the data collected by Narborough, he stressed the fact that the natives measured little over five feet, which is considered a normal height and proved the theory of the Patagonian giants to be false.

The English captain sailed towards the Estrecho de Magallanes and, in the Pacific Ocean, anchored near Valdivia, at a sensible distance from the Spanish cannons. But then he was forced to retire, abandoning four men and returning to England with very little to show for his efforts.

PATAGONIA

First it was Drake and then Cavendish, whose successful ventures around
the Strait set an example to be imitated by other pirates. Cavendish himself
returned again in 1592 with five ships and a crew of four hundred men. During
the voyage he assaulted every ship to be encountered between Africa and
Brazil. The city of Santos was ransacked by his people, and he had in mind
doing the same in Buenos Aires. But his purpose was defeated by a timely
storm that scattered the ships. The captains had established a meeting point
in Puerto Deseado, should any contingency arise; when they reunited once
again they advanced toward the Estrecho de Magallanes, only this time they
were not accompanied by favorable winds. Just storm and blizzard.
Cavendish, commanding the *Leicester*, reached Cape Froward. The crew,
desperate on account of the unbearable cold, rebelled. Cavendish had a
hostile relationship with his men, and on this occasion he was forced to
comply, thus returning to Brazil to wait for more favorable weather.

One of the five ships, called *Desire*, was commanded by John Davis, a
very expert navigator who wrote a full report of his experiences in both the
North and South Seas. Prior to Cavendish's departure, Davis had lost contact
with the other ships and was declared a deserter.

John Davis returned to the Estrecho de Magallanes following a route that
took him nearer Malvinas, but a storm prevented him from reaching the
Pacific. So he decided to return to Puerto Deseado. Most of his men were
either sick with scurvy or attacked by lice, and exhausted. And the ship was
badly in need of repair.

When both ship and crew were in fit condition to resume their expedition,
they headed for a region that is like a giant penguins' nest. Using wooden
poles they beat thousands of these birds to death, with the purpose of drying
and salting the meat. Around fifteen thousand penguins were thus stored in
the hold...and inflicted a worthy revenge on these brutal men: the meat had
worms, the kind of worm that devoured clothes, wood, even human flesh.
They were impossible to get rid of because they reproduced with terrifying
speed. And they produced an inflammatory disease that made the men
delirious and feverish, writhing in agony. The stench was unbearable. Only
John Davis and a young boy were uncontaminated.

What with diseases, an encounter with the *Tehuelches* which resulted in
the loss of nine men, another attack by natives and a Portuguese onslaught

which caused the death of thirteen sailors, the fact is that the original crew of seventy six men was reduced to only six.

Other English pirates imitating their predecessors were Andrew Merrick, John Chidley and Richard Hawkins, whose voyages in the vicinity of the Estrecho de Magallanes were also golden opportunities to assault whatever ships they met on the way.

And not only England produced fierce pirates. The Dutch, with the financial backing of rich, greedy bankers who reveled in the prospect of a profitable business with the gold and silver of Peru, had fully equipped fleets and were as cunning as they were brutal. Not only were they out to satisfy their personal ambition of riches and power, they were also interested in taking revenge on the Spanish invader.

Those financing these expeditions could rest at ease, their investments were quite safe: if, by any chance, the assault on Spanish ships leaving Peru was not too profitable, they could always make it up with the shipments of spices and various goods on the way back from the Molucas: nutmeg and sandalwood from Timor and Celebes, pepper, ginger, camphor, ebony and diamonds from Borneo and Sumatra; sugar, indigo, rum, tea and tobacco from Java; cinnamon from Ceylon; opium, silk and cotton from Bengal.

The English, on their side, went to India, where they were well looked upon because of their enmity with the Portuguese. The Company of the West Indies was beginning to expand and so did English commerce.

Robbing gold from Spanish ships and slave traffic brought enormous – and immediate- profits in gold, which was the currency at the time. That accounted for the large fortunes made by commercial companies, businessmen and members of the Court who, in turn, reinvested in new expeditions in this expanding sea market.

The affluence of gold could also be appreciated in commercial exchange between countries: for example, Spain purchasing manufactured goods from Holland, France, England and Italy. These countries furnished Spain with all sorts of merchandise, and strengthened their manufacturing industries in exchange for the gold which Spain thought would last forever. Thus, Spain chose good living and luxury while the other countries emphasized their working abilities and production .

The first Dutch fleet left the port of Gorée in June of 1598: five ships under the orders of Captain Jacobo Mahu. A few months after leaving port Mahu died and was replaced by Simón de Cordes.

The voyage was anything but peaceful. Frequent encounters with enemy ships made landing for supplies impossible. Hunger, thirst and scurvy were permanent and uninvited guests. When they finally reached Buenos Aires they were not allowed to land. That forced them to continue on their way to the Estrecho de Magallanes. Like most of these long expeditions to Patagonian lands, it resulted in disease, thirst, more than a hundred men who died or simply disappeared in a storm. Crossing to the Pacific was frustrated by another storm that scattered the ships. Of the five original ships, three disappeared and were never heard of again; the *Geelof* hid in the Strait, and another was captured by the Spaniards.

Three months after the departure of Jacobo Mahu´s fleet, four ships left port under the command of Oliver Van Noorth. During a stop at Deseado they fought against the *Tehuelches* and then continued on to the Estrecho de Magallanes. There they met the *Geelof*, commanded by Sebald de Weert, who thought he could join forces with Van Noorth. But, as the latter refused to give de Weert food for his crew, he angrily departed heading towards the Atlantic.

The lack of comradeship shown by Van Noorth towards his own fellow countrymen is difficult to understand. He was obviously a cruel, hard man. He continued sailing along the Pacific, landing in different points of Chile, Peru and Central America, looting and killing.

He became one of the most feared pirates in Spanish domains.

There were many other expeditions, all financed by important business concerns. In 1614, a fleet of six ships sailed, commanded by Joris Spilbergen, with the financial support of the Company of the West Indies.

Two other ships, *Concordia* and *Hoorn*, under the command of William Schouten, were equipped by another firm, a competitor of the West Indies Company. In this expedition, Jacobo Le Maire went as commercial agent.

Later expeditions had more ambitious objectives: after so many voyages of reconnaissance and discovery, the main interest was to establish Dutch colonies in Chile and Peru.

The Spaniards were just as scared of the Dutch expansion as they had been of the English. Specially since Schouten and Le Maire discovered a new crossing to the Pacific, through the Estrecho Le Maire and Cap Hoorn. Having control of the Estrecho de Magallanes now proved insufficient to stop pirates from other nations.

In a way, we can imagine that the Patagonian land was the scenario of a real war between European nations. All the expeditions were sent to conquer lands and riches for the glory of each particular country: England, Holland, Spain, France, they all fought mercilessly for a larger portion of power for their own mother country.

When the Spaniards realized that they had helped awaken the ambitious beast in all their European neighbors, they developed a new kind of obsession: at sea, they must protect their ships from the attacks of foreign pirates. And inland, they had to strengthen their defense and try to discover new sources of gold and silver and valuable goods. Seen from this angle, we could guess that colonization evolved, not so much as an aim on its own but as a way of self-defense.

Two centuries had elapsed since Magallanes´s voyage and still no signs of colonization in Patagonia. The first objective that Spain had in mind when sending the first expedition was finding a pass that would lead them to the Especiería islands. But then the discovery of gold and silver mines in Peru brought about a change in the original plans. The Estrecho de Magallanes attracted the most famous pirates from different nations who landed on the Patagonian coast to spend the winter, repair the ships and gather strength to continue on their dangerous but lucrative voyages. And that represented a major problem for Spain, who had to think of a way of fortifying that region. Otherwise, losing control could endanger the valuable cargo that fattened the ships going back home. Colonization of Patagonia had never been a part of the original scheme. It became necessary when other nations started to show special interest in expanding their power. Not only England, but also France, which established the first colony in the Malvinas (Malouines, name given to the islands by Louis Antoine de Bougainville in memory of Saint Malo) and the Dutch expeditions.

Nevertheless, the tragic attempts carried out by the first expeditions – Loaisa, Alcazaba, Sarmiento de Gamboa- could account for the lack of enthusiasm in the face of this new challenge.

Finding new sources of precious metals became a goal in itself, because the gold and silver mines in Peru had , to a great extent, been despoiled and were already well known as depots of valuable goods. Spanish ships leaving

Peru laden with riches attracted the attention of pirates of other nationalities and could be an easy prey to plunder.

Besides, greed was a powerful drive. Some expeditions had been carried out with the sole purpose of finding places like Trapalanda, or the Ciudad de los Césares, fabulous places which were the product of some feverish imagination, or maybe dreamed of in a moment of hallucination. Who knows...

In 1605 Hernandarias left for Neuquén to find the Ciudad de los Césares, taking with him eight hundred men, one thousand horses, carts and oxen, crossing deserts and desolate places under the blazing sun, occasionally fighting with the natives, and all this for nothing. He returned to Buenos Aires because his men were exhausted, but he never stopped believing in the existence of the mythical city. He just considered it was difficult to find.

In 1669 a priest, Father Nicolás Mascardi, founded a mission next to Lake Nahuel Huapi, and it has been rumoured that he carried out several journeys in the quest of the Ciudad de los Césares. He was killed by the natives, in Santa Cruz.

In the meantime, the English were still trying to establish a colony on the Patagonian coast. In 1669 two English ships, the *Sweepstake* and the *Batchelor Pink*, with a crew of a hundred men and under the command of Captain John Narborough, left port. The purpose of this voyage was a reconnaissance of the coastline, observing the habits and characteristics of the natives and promoting commercial relationships. It was agreed that if the ships separated during the voyage, they would meet again at Puerto Deseado.

The *Sweepstake* was the first to cast anchor, and, while waiting for the other ship, they began to grow a vegetable garden. John Narborough, tired of waiting for the *Batchelor Pink*, declared Port Desire (Deseado) and the barren lands surrounding it exclusive property of the English Crown. Once the English flag was blowing in the Patagonian wind, Narborough headed for San Julián in search of the other ship which was carrying tools and the necessary materials to build a naval station. They spent the winter there, under extremely hard living conditions. But Narborough was able to fulfil his assignment: contact with the *Tehuelches* allowed him to describe their ways and habits. And a detailed survey of the canals of Tierra del Fuego resulted in a map of the Strait that proved very valuable to future generations of seamen.

PATAGONIA

3.- JAMES COOK AND HIS SCIENTIFIC JOURNEY

French occupation of the "Malouines" – Spain appeals to a treaty and the French evacuate the islands – James Cook - The English watch over the strategic access to the Pacific – The origin of the Robinson Crusoe tale - Attempts to control the outlet to the Pacific

José de Andonaegui, Governor of the Río de la Plata, entrusted the Jesuits with the founding of a mission in Patagonia. The Jesuits appointed for this task were Matías Strobel, José Quiroga and José Cardiel, who left Buenos Aires in December of 1745, in the company of eight hundred men and under the command of Joaquín Olivares y Centeno.

In spite of the enthusiasm shown by all, Jesuits and laymen alike, this voyage was doomed –like so many others- to failure. Careful scrutiny of different points along the shore revealed that no place in Patagonia was fit to shelter a settlement, so the three priests and the crew returned to Buenos Aires defeated, after four months of dangerous sailing.

Spain was adamant in protecting the monopoly of its American colonies; nevertheless, all its efforts usually proved to be fruitless in view of the siege imposed by their adversaries in control of the sea; the freebooters had the upper hand of the situation and the Spaniards were powerless to stop smuggling.

In 1764 John Byron (grandfather of the famous poet), a high ranking official in the English Navy, left the port of Plymouth with two ships. Apparently, this expedition had scientific purposes and was to carry out a survey of the Patagonian coast. But in the end they did the same as other expeditions, which was to establish strategic positions along the route towards the East, specially in the vicinity of the Estrecho de Magallanes.

This was just another maddening advance against the Spaniards´ frustrated attempts to defend their domains.

Byron´s voyage lasted almost two years. During that time he made a thorough exploration of the Patagonian shores, the Estrecho de Magallanes and the Malvinas Islands, carried out the circumnavigation of Tierra del Fuego and reached the Pacific Ocean around the Cabo de Hornos. It was he who gave Punta Arenas its name: Sandy Point.

Occasionally there were expeditions with explicit scientific purposes. Such was the case of James Cook, cartographer, astronomer and mathematician, who commanded the merchant ship *Endeavour* on a voyage financed by the Royal Society of London. Partners in this expedition were a brilliant team of scientists representing different disciplines (botanists, naturalists, cosmographers and astronomers).

In a voyage around the world that lasted three years he observed the Patagonian coastline, Tierra del Fuego, the Isla de los Estados, and was the first to explore the Antarctic Polar Circle. He discovered the Sociedad archipelago, and many islands: Nueva Zelanda, Nueva Caledonia, the South Georgias (on the 17th of January 1775, naming them after King George I) and the Sandwich del Sur (christened in honor of John Montague, Earl of Sandwich, who became famous, not so much for his rank but for his creation: slices of cold cuts on hunks of bread to appease his hunger during gambling sessions).

Cook traveled all along the Pacific Ocean, leaving a detailed register of his studies in maps and travel diaries.

He also discovered the cure for scurvy, (a mixture of lemon, lime and raw vegetables) thus putting an end to one of the most feared diseases suffered by sailors in those days.

James Cook was most respected by his colleagues. In fact, the famous French navigator Dumont d´Urville acknowledged him as being "the best of the navigators and explorers of all times and of all nations".

James Cook died in 1779 during a native onslaught on one of the Hawaiian islands.

The "Malvinas" islands

During the first half of the XVIII Century, the Malvinas were frequented by navigators of different nationalities. Among them was the Englishman Woodes Rogers, a smuggler who became famous because he found the Scotsman Alexander Selkirk -on the island Juan Fernández,- dressed in rags and pieces of fur, dirty and unkempt, looking like a savage.

This primitive man had been a member of the crew on the ship

28

commanded by Stradling the pirate who, at the sailor´s first misdemeanor, left him stranded on an uninhabited island. As a parting gift he left him a rickety old cot, some tools and utensils, a weapon and a Bible. He had already been living on the island for over five years when Rogers found him, in a pitiable state and talking to himself. Thanks to Daniel Defoe Selkirk became a legend under the name of Robinson Crusoe.

Everybody was after the same thing: to occupy a strategic position that would enable control of the access to the Pacific Ocean and of the adjacent seas.

The French were the first to establish a naval station. In 1764 Louis Antoine Bougainville left Saint Malo commanding the ships *L´Aigle* and *Sphynx*, taking with him some settlers from the French part of Canada, a naturalist and a Benedictine monk called Dom Pernetty who was to write the chronicles of the expedition.

Stopping first at Montevideo to buy horses and cows, he finally took possession of the islands at a place they named Port Louis. The islands were christened Iles Malouines and hosted the first settlement: twenty-nine men, tools, seeds, weapons, supplies and the animals that would be the first breeds in the region.

On one of the many voyages to the Strait looking for wood Bougainville came across John Byron´s fleet. Byron had anchored in another place on the Malvinas which he named Port Egmont and built a fort leaving a garrison to guard it.

In the meantime, Port Louis was flourishing. Bougainville managed to attract another hundred and fifty-nine settlers who started growing new species and exported sealskins and oil to France.

Of course, the Spaniards were quick to react. After many tedious negotiations, Louis XV finally agreed to dissolve the French colony. In return, the Spanish Crown promised to compensate the French for their expenses and investments.

Bougainville was sorry to give up the Malvinas, because he, together with his farmers and artisans, had carried out an efficient and prosperous colonization process. Later on he launched on a round-the-world trip of which he kept written records in a book that became famous for its historical and scientific value.

Meanwhile John Byron, aware of the French colony in Port Louis, sent a ship to London bearing the news. The Admiralty immediately sent a ship – the *Jason*- under the orders of John Mac Bride, to inform the French that they were occupying English territory. More precisely, that the Falkland Islands belonged to the British Crown and the French had to leave without delay.

The French left quickly, which rather surprised the English. Of course, at first they did not know that they evacuated the islands because of the arrangement made with Spain and not because of Mac Bride´s warning.

When faced with the evidence that the Malvinas were coveted by France and England alike, the King of Spain ordered the Governor of Buenos Aires, Francisco de Paula Bucarelli, to establish a colony in Tierra del Fuego. To that end he sent captain Manuel Pando who, towards 1768, gave in a full report of his survey, pointing out Puerto Deseado as the most suitable place to settle on account of its varied fauna and its climate. Nevertheless, Bucarelli ordered other incursions around Tierra del Fuego and Malvinas with the purpose of keeping an eye on the region. He found no resistance until 1770, when he ordered the English to evacuate Port Egmont.

The English only left the islands in 1774, but they never gave up the idea of returning some day to establish a base.

The Spaniards had no difficulty in keeping control of Malvinas from 1774 until 1810.

4.- THOMAS FALKNER

The Jesuit Thomas Falkner warned that "any great power could secretly invade Patagonia" – He also alerted the Spaniards about an increasing number of foreign whalers and fishing boats – The Spanish Crown and its colonization plans as a way of defending its territory – Native onslaught on the colony of San José – Warfare between the Indians and the Spaniards – Viedma and the first settlement

In 1774 the Jesuit Thomas Falkner said that "if any nation should ever wish to inhabit these lands (Patagonia) it would only be a question of keeping the Spaniards in a continuous state of alarm…"

Such was the opinion of the author of the book "Descripción de la Patagonia y lugares adyacentes de Sur América". In view of which, the Spaniards were forced to admit that after two hundred and fifty years they had not been able to even establish an important base to protect their domains in that region.

But Falkner went even further when he said that that nation could proceed "with the utmost secrecy" and could "settle and occupy the place for years without the Spaniards ever finding out".

This was a subtle way of informing the English that setting foot in Patagonia would prove very easy thanks to Spanish incompetence.

The presence of foreign whaleboats and fishing vessels in South Atlantic waters made the Spaniards even more uneasy and they were finally driven to attempt some sort of colonization.

The usual Spanish bureaucracy was unable to delay the plans that had been presented to the King (Carlos III) by the Count of Floridablanca and had received full support.

The two resulting expeditions finally completed their mission at two points: in San José, a fort commanded by Antonio de Viedma, and the colony of Nuestra Señora del Carmen (Patagones), founded by his brother, Francisco de Viedma.

San José was surrounded by distrustful natives who resorted to assault tactics on the newcomers, and to stealing horses and cows. That was only the beginning of a series of disasters that ended in a brutal attack carried out by the Indians in August 1810, while mass was being celebrated: they burnt down the church and killed all the people they could find, including the priest, the surgeon and several soldiers. After taking nineteen prisoners with them, the Indians burnt down the whole village.

A few of the prisoners managed to escape and returned to Carmen de Patagones.

According to some of the chronicles, the attack carried out by the Indians was in retaliation for the cruel treatment they got from Antonio Aragón, who punished them with brutal beatings when he discovered any petty thieving.

Maybe his way of teaching them good manners...? The *Tehuelches* had their revenge in San José. The colony disappeared after the tragedy.

Floridablanca

Ever since Magallanes and Drake, San Julián was the customary stop all navigators used during their Patagonian voyages whenever they needed to rest, repair their ships or re-group if they happened to drift apart in the ocean. But it was not until 1780 that Antonio de Viedma was ordered to populate and fortify the bay.

He left Montevideo with soldiers, craftsmen, farmers, eight married couples, food stuff for a year, water for a few months, mules and tools. The *Tehuelches* gave them a warm welcome and their Indian chief, Julián, showed them around the place.

The big problem was drinking water. It was impossible to get it in San Julián, so they had to explore all the coast between Cabo Vírgenes and the Gulf of San Jorge. The expedition made a temporary stop at Deseado, as a precaution before the winter. There they settled temporarily, but harsh living conditions and scurvy caused many deaths and discontent among the people. That was the death sentence for this enterprise.

In a second attempt, a colony finally established itself in Cañadón de los Españoles. It was named Nueva Colonia de Floridablanca, and by the end of 1781 it consisted of chapel, fort, square, hospital, bakery, mill, workshop and even a pub. Also several houses, living quarters for one hundred and fifty settlers.

Even though they grew wheat and barley and bred cows, horses and mules, sheep, pigs and fowl, the food was not enough to meet the nutritional needs of the village.

In Buenos Aires, Viedma recommended Government support for Floridablanca, providing the population with whatever was necessary to survive and to eventually become a whaling port.

But Viceroy Vertiz was of the opinion that only self-sufficient colonies could survive. And, in that sense, Carmen de Patagones was the only colony that qualified in all the Patagonian coastline. So, in obedience to a decree issued by the Spanish Crown, complete destruction of Floridablanca was carried out, in January 1784.

Things were not easy in Carmen de Patagones either. It had just been founded when a flood obliged the people to move up river. On their return, they had to start all over again: the new village was named at first Las Piedras, then Mercedes de Patagones and finally, one hundred years later it was christened Viedma, in honor of its founder.

As from 1779 this colony attracted groups of immigrants from different parts of Spain: a large number of *Gallegos* were the first to arrive, then followed by others from Astorga, León, who were called *Maragatos*. Later on, that name would be applied to all inhabitants of Patagones.

In 1783 Viedma left Patagones; orders came that he was to assume higher responsibilities in Peru. Oddly enough, he was to be replaced by Juan de la Piedra, a controversial character who had committed serious blunders in San Julián and San José and had been accused of violating the mail that the Viedma brothers sent to the Viceroy. He was acquitted after a four-year trial and was sent to replace his successful and honored rival.

But he proved to be in keeping with his reputation: quite the contrary to Viedma, who was considerate and patient with the natives, de la Piedra was extremely cruel: slaying adults and children alike, he was using his brutal ways precisely in a place where the Indians reigned and outnumbered his forces; and just when the Indian chief Cacique Negro was negotiating peace with Viceroy Loreto in Buenos Aires.

He started a crazy war with the natives, where two brothers of Cacique Negro were killed.

Cacique Negro and another Indian chief Callfilqui, negotiated with Viceroy Loreto an indemnity for their dead, and an exchange of prisoners.

On the whole, the natives proved to be indulgent, allowing one hundred and fifty-seven prisoners to return to Carmen de Patagones.

But the clumsy attitude of Juan de la Piedra caused serious damage to Carmen de Patagones, depriving it of many inhabitants and about seven hundred horses which were necessary for rural work and as a means of transportation.

In view of the failure in establishing colonies along the Patagonian coast, the Crown proposed sending war ships which would explore and patrol the region. The first expedition to accomplish that mission was under the orders of Antonio de Córdoba, who left the port of Cádiz in 1785 in the ship *Santa María de la Cabeza*. He carried out a survey of the Estrecho de Magallanes and neighboring regions, and reached the conclusion that it was practically impossible to establish a colony with a minimum chance of success in what he considered was the most "wretched and unfortunate part of the Earth".

The next expedition was carried out by Alejandro Malaspina, who not only had to make a thorough reconnaissance of the region, he had also to write a confidential report on the political and social situation. For five years he visited all the important points between Buenos Aires and Tierra del Fuego, staying in all these places long enough to gather valuable cartographic information which he wrote down in a book that was never published. He established a friendly relationship with the *Tehuelches*, and bravely gave his personal opinion: he suggested allowing a "moderate emancipation" in America, and a "mild dependence on the Crown". He also considered that the delicate political situation in that part of the world was a result of the methods applied after the Conquest.

He paid dearly for his modern ideas: accused of rebellion against the Crown, he suffered imprisonment for eight years and was then banished to Italy.

Industrial Projects

Businessmen in Buenos Aires also laid eyes on Patagonia as an interesting financial target.

Salt mines in San Julián were valuable for the meat salting business and fishing also offered interesting prospects.

The Crown considered giving facilities to those who had industrial projects for Patagonia, because it would be an indirect way of keeping control of their domains and avoiding the trespassing of foreign ships.

King Carlos IV was induced into creating the Royal Maritime Company for the exploitation of the fishing industry in all its process: capture, salting and oil manufacture. A Royal Bill decreed the factory must be installed in Puerto Deseado.

Once again the Spaniards tried to establish a new colony, and in 1790 four ships left port carrying people, tools and building materials. They built some houses and basic premises and tried –unsuccessfully- to grow an orchard and vegetable garden. Like in so many other cases, scurvy and other diseases caused many deaths and desertions.

The meager production of skins, salt and oils was transported by ships. And barter with the *Tehuelches* provided them with *guanaco* meat, local fruits and hides.

But the Spaniards were very inefficient administrators and this enterprise, so promising at first, resulted in another failure. All the better for the English fishing ships which established a profitable commerce with the factory.

During the English Invasions of Buenos Aires, the factory was closed down. In October of 1907 the settlers were taken to Patagones. And that was the end of the Royal Company: only its ruins remained.

The desolate geography of these southern lands and its implacable climate are a severe handicap when it comes to establishing a colony. To this we must add the inefficiency of the Spanish Crown´s representatives. Thus, the only thing they had to show after three hundred years of Spanish dominion was the colony in Carmen de Patagones and an insignificant base in Puerto Soledad. Barely fifty people between soldiers, kin and prisoners were settled in Malvinas, fighting against the wind, the storms and the constant menace of North American fishing vessels that assaulted the village, stole their animals and killed the whales indiscriminately. In January 1811 the Spaniards finally abandoned Malvinas.

5.- PATAGONES UNDER THE REVOLUTIONARY GOVERNMENT OF MAY

Carmen de Patagones was the only continental settlement in Patagonia at the onset of the Government of May – The town was faithful to the Crown and opposed the Revolution – Resistance groups led a bloody warfare against the authorities – Patagones, den of freebooters – Brazilian naval invasion was defeated by freebooters, soldiers, settlers, farmers and former African slaves

The authorities derived from the May Revolution assumed their governmental responsibilities in Carmen de Patagones and in July 1810 named Captain Xavier de Sancho Commanding Officer. Unfortunately, Sancho was the least indicated person for that post: in the first place, because he was inefficient in his job; and secondly, because he was totally ignorant of the basics of diplomacy that would have been necessary to maintain a cordial relationship with the people, who were still loyal to the Crown.

The inhabitants of Carmen de Patagones were mostly Spanish. And faithful to the Spanish tradition, marriage between cousins was most usual. All fervent Catholics, very hard-working and used to putting up with difficult living conditions.

In September 1810 a group of royalists who had rebelled against the new government in Mendoza came to Patagones as prisoners.

Due to its geographic situation, surrounded by desert and hostile Indians and unable to escape by sea, Patagones was the ideal place to recruit political prisoners and deserters, lodging them in its fort.

Eventually the royalists, supported by the other prisoners in the fort – between them they outnumbered the troops that had them in custody- and by the remaining population, rebelled against the local authorities. They took over the fort, flew the Spanish flag and took Sancho prisoner naming the royalist Domingo Fernández in his place.

They sent messengers to Viceroy Vigodet, in Montevideo, letting him know that they had overturned the revolutionary government and recaptured power for the Crown.

The new *Criollo* Government was not going to accept defeat easily, and sent Lieutenant Coronel Oliver Russell plus one hundred soldiers to overturn Fernández.

Fernández left without putting up a fight.

Several disastrous governments and ensuing revolts made progress impossible in Patagones until the Government finally appointed José Gabriel de Oyuela Commanding Officer. This marked the beginning of a period of progress and prosperity.

These are some of his initiatives:

· He carried out a census, which revealed there were 471 inhabitants in Patagones.
· With the help of Bernardino Rivadavia, he founded the first school in August 1821.
· The organization of a postal service.
· The organization of a harbor pilot service
· Regulation of hunting and fishing, and establishing a fee.
· He made up for the ill-treatment shown by previous commanders towards the Indians and made an effort to maintain an amiable relationship with the local tribes.

In 1823 Oyuela was replaced by Martín Lacarra, who continued the work of his predecessor.

Lacarra was also in command of a garrison that was in a permanent state of alert, not only on account of the always possible Indian onslaught, but also because of the threat of war with Brazil. Which was, in fact, declared on the 2nd of April 1826, against the Provincias Unidas del Río de la Plata.

Brazil had several combat ships and privateers. The Provincias Unidas had very few ships and also hired the services of privateers, who obtained their license in exchange for the promise of supporting the nation´s naval operations against any attacking party.

Brazil blockaded the port of Buenos Aires, so the privateers established their operative base in Carmen de Patagones. A famous privateer, Francisco Fourmartin, used to leave this port on the ship *Lavalleja*, and he captured around forty Brazilian vessels.

The fierce attacks caused by the privateers were one of the reasons why the imperial forces wanted to destroy Patagones.

Thus, Patagones presented a bizarre contrast: on the one hand it was a colony of law-abiding and hard-working people, and on the other hand, it was

PATAGONIA

soon invaded by mercenaries, sailors of doubtful reputation, adventurers and African ex- slaves who were freed after the capture of Brazilian ships. There was wine and food in quantity, also gold and different merchandise that were not able to reach Buenos Aires on account of the Brazilian blockade and the Indian siege.

The prisoners in the fort outnumbered by far the forty-four soldiers that guarded them. Lacarra desperately needed more soldiers and weapons. But it was not easy to contact Buenos Aires. Communications were by sea, or on horseback: couriers who maybe rode one or two weeks trying to avoid the siege imposed by the Indians.

But Buenos Aires never sent the reinforcements, and Lacarra had to find solutions on his own. James Harris, privateer and captain of the ship *Hijo de Mayo*, assured Lacarra that with some help and craftsmen he could build a battery with four cannons to protect the mouth of the river. Lacarra promptly gave him workers and 3.245 pesos.

The Brazilians were aware of Patagones´ military weakness and decided that its downfall was imminent. Their squadron, under the command of Captain James Shepherd, had a clear objective which was, according to documents of the Imperial War Ministry:

> *"to get hold of, and demolish the battery of the port of Patagones, destroy the village and to capture or burn down the ships there anchored (thus) depriving Buenos Aires of its only remaining port, establishing commerce with the Pampas and convincing them to renew their assaults around Buenos Aires"*

On February 1827 the Imperial Fleet reached the mouth of the river (Río Negro).

Lacarra knew he lacked the means to organize a proper defense. Once in power, Bernardino Rivadavia sent Coronel Felipe Pereyra and two officers to help Lacarra in organizing the troops. A hundred African ex-slaves freed by the privateers would also help to integrate a company. Pereyra also brought with him some soldiers and weapons.

From Bahía Blanca, Coronel Rauch commissioned José Luis Molina and twenty-two *gauchos* under his command, to try to obtain Indian support against the Brazilians. At first Lacarra had doubts about Molina because of his bad reputation (he married an Indian, lived with the tribe and commanded several *malones* -Indian raids-, destroying whole villages, stealing cattle and taking women and children captive). But eventually Molina fell out of grace with the tribe and requested the army´s protection and a pardon from the Government. Which he got and, in return, used his skills as a guide in the desert he knew so well, and his knowledge of the Indian ways, to collaborate in the rescue of around three hundred women and children held captive in the Indian camps.

Although nobody trusted him completely, his skills were valuable at this time when cunning and clever slyness would have to make up for the lack of material means in organizing a defense against the Imperial forces.

Commander Lacarra managed to assemble a company of one hundred and fifty infantry, a cavalry squadron of around one hundred men, two hundred privateers –mostly foreigners- and townspeople and an artillery picket.

The privateer ships ready for combat were the *Hijo de Julio*, commanded by Fourmantin, the *Hijo de Mayo*, under the orders of the English privateer James Harris and the brig *Oriental Argentino*, commanded by the Frenchman Pierre Dautant.

Commanding the Argentine Navy was a Welshman called Santiago Jorge Bynon on board the *Bella Flor*. The chronicles say that Bynon launched against the *Escudero* which –like the other ships of the Brazilian fleet- was flying the Argentine flag. The trick didn´t deceive Coronel Felipe Pereyra, in charge of the battery at the mouth of the river. He ordered to fire at the *Escudero* and the *Itaparica*, causing some damage. But when the battery remained without ammunition it was destroyed by the powerful imperial ships.

The hundred Africans under Pereyra´s orders went on fighting, shooting against the ships until they ran out of ammunition. Obviously, they had made up their minds to kill or die, but never to become slaves again.

In the meantime, the *Duquesa de Goyaz* had stranded and the *Itaparica* shipwrecked in a storm. Bynon thought the time was just right for the final blow and proposed an immediate attack. He was supported by Ambrosio Mitre and authorized by Coronel Lacarra. Before an hour had elapsed Bynon had captured the *Escudero*, while Harris successfully attacked the *Constancia*. The Argentine naval force, strengthened by the captured ships, finally charged against the *Itaparica*, now unable to resist the enemy attack.

The invaders had no luck inland either.

The defenders –some on horseback and others hiding among the bushes-launched a surprise attack on four hundred Brazilians in Cerro de la Caballada.

PATAGONIA

And in the meantime, hundreds of army caps appeared over the edge of the fort walls. This was only a trick meant to deceive the invaders. What they thought was an impressive display of military power was really a large number of women and children wearing army caps....

As for Molina and his *gauchos,* they resorted to a typical Indian trick, which was to set fire to the pastures. Suffocated by the smoke and exhausted, the Brazilians scattered and became an easy prey for Second Lieutenant Olivera and his soldiers.

Other chronicles also referred to thirst as a major problem for the demoralized Brazilians. It actually drove them to lick the horses' sweat.

Final results of this war were:
- The Argentine fleet increased its power with three ships captured from the enemy.
- More than five hundred and fifty soldiers and sailors and approximately twenty officers were taken prisoner. The Argentines summed up a total of sixteen casualties.
- In both attempts to destroy the "nest of privateers", the Brazilian Empire had sacrificed almost one thousand men and lost six ships.

Carmen de Patagones assembled privateers, soldiers, austere settlers, ex slaves, craftsmen, *Gauchos* and townspeople in a strange group that, in spite of having scarce ammunition, few ships and old weapons, managed to defeat the enemy in one brave, resounding victory.

And thus, in march of 1827, this distant republican bastion became a part of History.

Curiously enough, the floods proved to be an implacable enemy. The inhabitants of Patagones suffered several devastating floods.

Which proves that sooner or later, nature leaves its powerful hallmark in all Patagonian lands.

6.- EXPEDITIONS OF PARKER KING AND FITZ ROY

Important expeditions were carried out by commanders Parker King and Robert Fitz Roy – Darwin and his controversial opinion of Patagonia – Natives of Tierra del Fuego were taken to England and presented at Court –English missionaries and their tragic end – An Indian Chief sold the Estrecho de Magallanes to an Irishman

English expeditions commanded by Philip Parker King (1826 and 1830) and Robert Fitz Roy (1832 and 1836) to explore and survey produced very valuable information about the Patagonian coasts, all of which was recorded in interesting stories.

Parker King left the port of Plymouth in March 1826 with two ships, the *Adventure* and the *Beagle*. They reached the Strait in 1827, stopping near Port Famine (name that Cavendish gave the place originally called Rey Felipe). After an exhaustive study of the region for almost three years they discovered the Beagle Canal.

When they were near Navarino Island, the *Yaganes* stole a whaling ship from them. With the idea of teaching them a lesson, the English took four hostages on board. Another version says they kept them in order to observe them and then train them as interpreters so they could later influence their people. The fact is the four *Yaganes* went to England and were christened Fuegia Basket (the only girl), Jemmy Button (because the price paid for him was a huge mother-of-pearl button), Boat Memory (in memory of the lost boat) and York Minster (the place where they had been captured).

Fitz Roy was responsible for all expenses, including their education. They became so famous in England that they were received by King William IV and Queen Adelaide, who gave them many valuable gifts. For instance, Fuegia was given a complete wedding outfit and a very fine cap that belonged to the Queen herself.

Fitz Roy, the Beagle, Darwin

The voyage of Fitz Roy on board the Beagle began in December 1831. With him traveled Charles Darwin, because Fitz Roy had wanted a naturalist on his team. At the time Darwin was only a twenty-three-year-old natural science student, and he was quite willing to travel without charging a fee. Another travel companion was the Reverend Richard Matthews, whose purpose was to teach the Indians Christian religion and convert them.

Of the four Indian captives only three returned. Boat Memory had died of smallpox (Fitz Roy was particularly sorry because he was the best looking and the most intelligent of the lot). They had been taught different trades: carpentry, blacksmith, farming. And the English language. York Minster was twenty-six when he was taken captive and he was engaged to Fuegia Basket. He was not particularly keen on learning.

During their stay in England, the *Yaganes* had lived in a town called Wathanstown and when returning to Tierra del Fuego their neighbors gave them many presents: clothes, food supplies, tools for their folks back home and… books and chinaware to set the table.

In December 1832 Fitz Roy reached Wulaia, on the island of Navarino, the same place he had visited three years back. The *Yaganes* stayed there with their families, but living in huts: Jemmy in a hut all to himself, and Fuegia Basket and York Minster (who had been married by the Reverend Matthews) in another.

The newly arrived began tilling the earth and sowing seeds, applying the knowledge they had acquired in England. The other *Yaganes* used to approach them and watch. One day they were visited by Jemmy´s mother and brothers but they were very distant and barely exchanged a few words.

Some weeks later Fitz Roy returned from his reconnaissance work and found Reverend Matthews depressed and scared. The natives had attacked him with stones and they made fun of him pulling his beard and making frightening gestures while dancing around him. In the end they robbed him of all his things. The *Yaganes* had paid no heed to Jemmy Button, who pleaded and begged them to leave him alone. Reverend Matthews described the natives as "rude savages". Shortly after he left Wulaia and returned home with the others.

In a later stage of the expedition they made a survey of San Julián and the river Santa Cruz. Fitz Roy had the intention of finding the source of this river. Travelling with him were Charles Darwin and twenty-four sailors in three boats.

This proved to be quite a risky adventure. Going up-river was tiresome and dangerous, because the more they advanced the stronger the current and the moment came when oars were useless. They had to walk and tow the boats, but even walking became more strenuous. Sometimes they came across some islets with thorny bushes and had to drag themselves in tow through the thicket.

They were most intrigued at the discovery of small foot prints marked on the muddy banks and disappearing into the river. Obviously it meant that women and children crossed the river. But then, they wondered, how could they possibly find the strength to wade across two hundred yards with such strong currents? How did they manage it, considering there was no wood nor rushes to build rafts?

They came across these traces quite often, and occasionally they felt observed by the natives although they were never able to actually discover or see them.

Maybe the answer to this mystery lies in the testimony of the Paraguayan native Hilário Tapary, who, after leaving San Julián on a long journey to Buenos Aires, stopped to rest in an Indian camp. He said that the natives, about a hundred Indians, had to cross a river with strong currents. And they did so using some leather balls which transported the men and their families plus their tents. These balls were tied with leather straps to horses –specially trained to wade the river- and they were towed safely to the opposite side.

If they had no horses, then the men would swim across the river towing the leather balls with the straps between their teeth.

Fitz Roy and the English sailors were eventually able to see, at a distance, the snow peaked mountains of the Cordillera de los Andes.

But, to their disappointment:

> *"For three days we had been advancing towards these distant mountains* –wrote Fitz Roy- *which, at times, were clearly visible; but this morning the distance seemed as long as the day when we first saw their snowcapped peaks"*

After eighteen days of walking he ruefully decided to return. He christened that site Valle del Misterio (Mystery Valley). Thanks to the powerful currents, it took him only three days to cover the distance to the parting point by boat.

Fitz Roy never found out that he had been only thirty miles away from his objective.

The records resulting from these surveys were most valuable, and some of the references can be found in the book Darwin published in 1839 "Diary of a Naturalist Around the World".

Darwin often wondered why it was that the Patagonian plains were considered by most as wretched and useless; why were they only well known by all that is negative: no inhabitants, no water, no trees, no mountains. Why then -and he said he was not the only one- did these barren lands possess his mind? Why was it that the green, fertile *pampa* that people found so useful, did not produce in him the same impression? He could not fully understand the reason, but he thought it might partly be because "this barren land enhances the horizons of imagination".

On their return several months later, they were surrounded in the Beagle Canal by many canoes full of *Yaganes*. Among them was Jemmy Button, looking unkempt, very thin, his hair long, and almost naked, saluting so that they would recognize him. They invited him aboard and asked him to clean up and put on sailors´ clothes. He sat at table with the officers and Captain Fitz Roy, using knife and fork and displaying his best table manners.

After dinner Jemmy told that they had abandoned the wooden huts they had built -on the style of those in northern Europe-, because they were much too high and that made them very cold. The English duly took note of this. He also told how York Minster built a big canoe and left taking Fuegia Basket with him after creeping into his hut and stealing all his belongings.

On hearing these stories Fitz Roy was very upset. Together with the Revd. Matthews, he had just about given up hope of civilizing the *Yaganes*. Maybe when these sad things happened he would be haunted by the tales told to him by the young *Yaganes* during the trip to Europe. Like when they described the way they ate some occasional enemy, or even the old women of the tribe. Besides, he was aware that Darwin believed these Indians were cannibals, an opinion shared by Van Noort and other members of Sarmiento de Gamboa´s expedition. On the contrary, Lucas Bridges believed this idea of cannibalism among the *Fueguinos* was totally untrue.

Before leaving, Jemmy Button made a gift of some otter skins to his friends on the *Beagle*. And he presented Fitz Roy with a bow and arrows and a harpoon made by himself.

As a farewell parting gesture, when the ship was leaving he made a bonfire.

The smoke would be visible for a long time.

Later reference of Jemmy Button figured in the dramatic report made by Alfred Cole, cook on the ship *Allen Gardiner*, which took missionaries of the Patagonian Missionary Society to Wulaia.

One morning, one of the missionaries, Garland Phillips, disembarked with the idea of celebrating mass for three hundred *Yaganes*. Alfred Cole was idly looking on, and suddenly a gesture made by some Indians drew his attention. He saw them grab the oars of the boat transporting the eight missionaries and throw them into the water. After which they hit the sailor on the head with a blunt object. Screaming wildly, they attacked the clergymen, who desperately ran towards the sea. The natives caught up with them and beat them to death. Then they climbed on board the ship to loot and Cole managed to escape in a rowboat.

The cook hid for a few days in the thicket but when he was driven by hunger out of his shelter he was discovered by the natives, who captured him but let him live.

Captain W. H. Smiley went to rescue the missionaries and was dismayed when he heard about the massacre. He found the cook almost out of his mind, on account of the terrible memories that haunted him and also because of his dramatic existence living with the natives.

The bodies were never found, and Alfred Cole accused Jemmy Button of having instigated the murders.

The sale of the Estrecho de Magallanes

In 1845, an Irishman who worked as harbor pilot in the Strait actually bought the famous passage discovered by Fernando de Magallanes. This fantastic operation was due to the offensive treatment given by the Chileans to the *Tehuelches*, who, wounded in their pride, commissioned the famous Indian chief Casimiro Biguá to carry out the sale.

No information of this sale is registered, and nobody knows the identity of the Irishman.

Rumors spread in Montevideo; word also got around to Patagones and even Buenos Aires, where Rosas made England responsible for the extravagant operation: he denied Casimiro authority and annulled the sale.

Casimiro and his *Tehuelches* considered themselves the rightful owners of the Strait and the area around it.

When Casimiro was just a young boy his father died fighting against the *Araucanos*. His mother promptly took him to Patagones and exchanged him for a barrel of rum. The child's "owner" was no other than the ex-privateer Fourmantin, also called Bivois or Biguá, governor of Patagones and then head of the Buenos Aires squadron. Casimiro was still just a teenager when he went back to the Indian camp in the Estrecho de Magallanes.

And as to the Irishman who bought the Strait, he made a profitable business charging one pound per ton of *guano* deposited in his warehouse; he had the necessary staff to help store the mounds of *guano* that ships left in his care in the anchoring grounds.

More data concerning this unusual character can be found in the chronicles written by Lieutenant C. Skogman aboard the Swedish frigate *Eugenia*, during its voyage around the Rio de la Plata and the southern coastline.

They felt most curious about the famous "gigantic" Patagones, but they were unable to find them. Strangely enough, they were favored by good weather, and a succession of calm, sunny days. They were surprised by the lack of trees.

When they reached the Strait they looked around for the harbor pilot that was to guide them on their course, and it was not until reaching the first strait that they discovered the news: there were five ships loading *guano*. According to Skogman, he once saw up to ten ships loading *guano* at the same time.

The Swedes were rather confused and went on their way up to a Chilean colony where they were once again shaken: in the harbor there were twenty-five dead animals, all half rotten, the air full of the most awful stench. A group of criminals had assaulted the colony and there were signs of fighting inside the huts, furniture and beds destroyed, food strewn on the floor, clothing and blankets in tatters. The writer did not mention finding any dead bodies, but he did say there were very neat orchards and vegetable gardens that were obviously well looked after.

The crew of the *Eugenia* disembarked in order to bury one of the sailors who had died on board, in an accident. It just so happened that in that cemetery was the tomb of the English officer Pringle Stokes, of the *Beagle*. They paid homage to his memory.

When they were finally ready to leave they saw a ship approaching, carrying the most fearsome looking men, in chains. These were some of the criminals that had raided the colony and had been taken prisoner.

All these events were too shocking for the Swedes, who proceeded on their journey, fully convinced that these lands were risky and dangerous and that, therefore, the sooner they got away, the better.

The sky, gray and ominous, seemed to match the darkness in their hearts.

7.- LUIS PIEDRA BUENA

Luis Piedra Buena was a bold navigator who was trained by North American sea-lion hunters – He was a zealous guardian of maritime sovereignty and appropriately called "Sentinel of the South" – He risked his life in countless opportunities – He saved more than two hundred shipwrecked people and was duly acknowledged by the Queen of England and the Kaiser of Germany

Luis Piedra Buena was born in Carmen de Patagones on the 23rd of August 1833. As a child, he was always fascinated by the stories and adventures of privateers and sea-lion hunters. His vocation was therefore linked to the sea and its mysteries. And maybe that is the reason why, at the age of only nine, he began his life at sea as cabin boy in the ship belonging to Captain F. Lennon, under whose guidance he learnt the secrets of the trade.

Three years later he accompanied Captain William H. Smiley, well-known North American whaler, on his voyages along the Atlantic coastline and nearby islands until reaching the Antarctic peninsula. He proved to be quick at learning the art of catching whales and seals, and, in fact, he was such an accomplished sailor that Smiley decided to pay for his tuition at a school specializing in nautical training, in New York.

(There was no training school for sailors in Argentina, and it was only in 1872 that Domingo Faustino Sarmiento founded the Escuela Naval Militar. Until then, Argentina used to hire the services of foreign sailors, both military and privateers, and with them improvised the naval force that intervened after the independence battles. Some *Criollos* trained with Brown, Bouchard, Drummond, Fournier, Azopardo, Laserre, Murature, Py, Robinson, Seaver, Thorne, Spiro, Grandville, among other famous seamen).

Three years later Luis Piedra Buena got his master´s ticket, with a general knowledge of nautical carpentry and mechanics, and returned to Argentina.

Very soon he would start to work on his own, in an effort to link his sailing activity with some commercial project.

In 1859 he set up a general store on the small island Fitz Roy had named Islet Reach and that he re-named Pavón in honor of the battle fought by

Bartolomé Mitre. There he built his living quarters, a warehouse and other departments. His clients were the local Indians and the occasional travelers that would pass by to buy supplies (food, tobacco, *yerba,* sugar) in exchange for feathers, hides and *quillangos* (a fur rug).

But he was not a passive salesman. He was usually out sailing, so he used to leave some employee in charge of running the store.

Piedra Buena was a man of enterprise, but he was not always successful. He once installed a factory for processing penguin oil in the Isla de los Estados but it was a huge failure and the ship foundered.

Piedra Buena was aware of the powerful influence the Chileans had over the Indians. He therefore traveled to Buenos Aires taking with him the Indian chief Casimiro and introduced him to Bartolomé Mitre, who appointed him "Principal Chief of the Patagonian coast up to the extreme of the Andean Range".

Casimiro was convinced that his new nomination was more important than that of simple captain of the Chilean army which he had until then. When the Governor of Punta Arenas found out about his "desertion" he stopped his salary.

The Government in Buenos Aires finally began to consider Piedra Buena´s warning concerning Chilean influence and the need to defend Argentine sovereignty in Patagonia. Following his instructions, the Englishman G. H. Gardner explored the Santa Cruz river. Coasting the river on horseback and with the aid of two *peones* (rural laborers) it took them thirty-three days to reach the lake where the river originated; they made a survey of the region and Piedra Buena sent the reports to the Ministry of Foreign Affairs.

In 1869 he set up another general store in Punta Arenas. Then he built a shelter for shipwrecked victims on the Isla de los Estados and another in San Gregorio, but the Chileans demanded he pull them down.

Even though the Chileans followed his every move in Punta Arenas, they couldn´t help feeling a certain respect for his professionalism. He was famous for his skill as a sailor and for his solidarity towards all those who chose the difficult life at sea.

He rescued many ships and saved almost two hundred lives. People showed their gratitude in different ways. Sometimes he received valuable gifts, like the binoculars given to him by the Queen of England, or the telescope sent to him by the German Emperor.

Nevertheless, gossip and slander in Punta Arenas did him a lot of harm. The Argentine Ambassador in Chile, Félix Frías, told all sorts of lies about Piedra Buena in Buenos Aires: that he was full of debts and unable to pay them, that he owned a pub with a bad reputation where he sold to the Indians all that the Argentine Government sent him as donations, or that he kept for his personal use stuff meant for local welfare, and so forth. He ended his report to the Ministry of Foreign Affairs objecting to his position as an officer in the Navy.

This campaign against his prestige -instigated by Oscar Viel, Governor of Punta Arenas-, resulted in a ban on any commercial enterprise in that Chilean city. As a consequence his general store, which used to be a prosperous concern, became practically worthless.

It was bought for pennies in 1876 by José Menéndez, who began his commercial activities in this region. We could say it was the starting point of one of the largest fortunes in the South of Chile.

Luis Piedra Buena, now on his own, had only the loyal support of his wife, Julia Dufour.

In February 1873 Piedra Buena was sailing on the *Espora* right in front of the Isla de los Estados, when a storm wrecked the ship in Bahía de las Nutrias. He waited and waited, his eyes gazing fixedly on the horizon, on the lookout in case some ship could be seen, somebody coming to rescue them...After some days of idle waiting he decided to build a cutter. With the aid of four men of his crew (the other four sailors were sick), a couple of saws and an ax they built a twelve-meter-long boat which was named *Luisito*.

Sixteen days later they anchored in Punta Arenas.

The example set by this man inspired an Englishman called Henry L. Reynard to write to the newspaper *Navy*:

> "*Don Luis Piedra Buena, whose noble conduct not only honors him but also the nation that has men as courageous and humanitarian as the one we now speak of (...) managed to save his crew from an almost inevitable death, assembled the remains of the Espora using some of them to build a warehouse to shelter his sailors from the island´s cruel climate and, finally, with uncommon creativeness, built, with the remaining pieces, the cutter that would take them to*

land safe and sound."

Reynard highlights the dangerous situations overcome by Piedra Buena and comments that they would make a book "far more interesting than many of the novels that are just a product of the writer's fantasy".

This Englishman was the first to bring sheep from Malvinas, thus proving they had no difficulty in adjusting to the Patagonian land. He promoted sheep raising, which would in the future be one of the main activities in that area.

Meanwhile, in Cañadón Misioneros, the Chileans established a base on the southern coast of the Santa Cruz river, using this point as a harbor for their own warships.

When authorities in Buenos Aires realized the real danger of a possible clash with Chile they sought Piedra Buena's advice, because no one knew the patagonian South as well as he did.

He was so efficient in carrying out this task that Félix Frías himself was moved to acknowledge it:

> *"Your report has been of enormous value to me. Patriots like*
> *yourself will, sooner or later, have their due reward."*

Chilean harassment led to many reconnaissance voyages to Patagonia, and Piedra Buena was the man chosen as guide and consultant in different cases. For instance, with the Lieutenant Carlos María Moyano and the "Perito" Moreno.

He used his ship *Santa Cruz* as a training base for troops which he instructed personally.

In 1878 President Avellaneda named him Colonel of the Navy, but Luis Piedra Buena didn't much care for a bureaucratic post. He continued to be "the sentry of the South Seas".

His last job was guiding the mission of the Instituto Geográfico Argentino commanded by Giacomo Bove, in an expedition that lasted eight months.

Piedra Buena, from his sickbed, gave instructions as to the placing of beacons in the Le Maire Strait.

He died some days later, at the age of fifty one.

In an obituary published by La Nación, this newspaper stated:

> *"It is a fact that the recovery of the southern territories of the*
> *Argentine Republic was, for the most part, due to Commander*
> *Piedra Buena's patriotism and the eagerness with which he carried*

out his task. He was the first to draw attention to these lands and we might say that, for a long time, he defended them on his own, with his small boat, always sailing through the straits, always watching, like a sentry of the seas. His passion was to defend this region and block all attempts of foreign occupation."

Once again Reynard wrote about Piedra Buena, and said he didn't know what he admired most in him: whether his skill as a shipbuilder, or his courage, or maybe his perseverance when accomplishing the difficult and perilous feats that were his aim in life.

Rescuing a ship, which was Piedra Buena's specialty, was most dangerous, not only because any action in those harsh waters is difficult in itself, but also because he was up against a racket of the times, the *raqueros*. These were like inland pirates, who hid in Malvinas on the lookout for a ship in danger. When the situation arose they would negotiate the rescue for a fee, which was usually equivalent to looting all they could lay their hands on. If the ship was in danger of capsizing they didn't even bother to negotiate....

So, for Piedra Buena it was a question of getting to the ship before the *raqueros* did, which very often meant interrupting his work. Quite the opposite to these sea gangsters, he never got any financial benefit. For him it wasn't business, it was just an act of solidarity.

Chatwin, after consulting reports, journalistic articles and even political accusations, reached the conclusion that the rescue department in José Menéndez's business concern was "similar to piracy". Which enhances even more Piedra Buena's rich personality and generous nature.

Always ready to give a helping hand, to watch over his country's interests, to rescue anyone in an emergency at sea, with no personal gain, and sometimes at great personal sacrifice. He suffered the loss of his eldest son, Luisito, then his wife died -at the age of forty-one- of consumption, a blow from which he never recovered completely.

History will remember him as a man who put the wellbeing of his country and his fellow men above all personal interests.

8.- AN EXTRAVAGANT MONARCHY

Orllie Antoine I, self-proclaimed King of Araucania and Patagonia – He was still in Périgueux, France when it occurred to him that he could civilize the Indians by becoming their chief – He escaped from pursuers who doubted his sanity and insisted that France would have profited from his realm

Ever since Magallanes discovered the Strait, Patagonia became a scenario for dramatic episodes. Nevertheless, there were also extravagant events, like the chapter of the famous "king".

On the 17th of November 1860 a Frenchman, Orllie Antoine de Tounens decided to travel to the legendary Araucania and become king. Among others, one of the reasons for this rather peculiar decision was that he had read the poem "La Araucana" by Alonso de Ercilla and, seduced by this epic tale, exchanged his humdrum existence in Périgueux for a life of adventure in Araucania.

He arrived –he was thirty-one at the time- and immediately got in touch with different Indian chiefs or *caciques*. His intention was to unite them under his reign in a constitutional monarchy.

> *"In the year 1860 I conceived the idea that the Indians could be civilized if I became their chief. My title could be King, or any other as long as it meant being the supreme power in a state. To that effect I went to the province of Valdivia or south of Araucania and contacted several Indian chiefs letting them know of my plans; as they seemed pleased to accept me and I, on the other hand, believed that the authority of a King is the most respected among them, I took that title".*

He made the *caciques* swear on the Constitution that would rule the new monarchy and then, in a solemn ceremony, the new subjects exclaimed "!Long live the King!". In any case, the new King was most disappointed because during the ceremony his new subjects did not take off their hats. So, talking through his interpreter, Rosales, he let them know that in the future they had to either uncover their heads if they had a hat on, or otherwise salute with their right hand. They cheered him and saluted him, doing as they were told.

Word got around, and he was supported by certain fellow countrymen living in Chile who were convinced that Orllie Antoine I was conquering lands for France.

In France there were groups of nationalists who feared their country would become overpopulated by the lower classes and welcomed the idea of transferring them to the colonies. Orllie Antoine therefore asked for a loan, with the idea of "inviting" the commoners and communists and all those who conspired against the "law and order" of his country to live in his *Araucano* kingdom.

Convinced that the Patagonian Indians would consider they had the same rights as the *Araucanos* and that they would also like to be subjects in his kingdom, he decided to expand his realm. However, the new king had no means, not even a proper army to achieve his new purpose.

So he did then what rulers usually do in these cases: he invented a conflict and declared war on Chile. But he was double-crossed by his guide, Rosales, and arrested by the Chilean authorities who didn´t know quite what to do with this intruder. The judge, believing him crazy, demanded a medical examination but the doctors declared him absolutely sane. The public prosecutor demanded that Orllie Antoine be executed as punishment for "disturbing public order". The French consul, Cazotte, afraid of what could happen to his fellow countryman, declared him insane and managed to ship him back to France. Meanwhile, he reported back to the Minister of Foreign Affairs, stating that

> "a Frenchman that calls himself Prince of Tounens is a strange character, half funny, half serious; he acts the part of a grave, reserved person. He once lived among the Indian tribes of Araucania and proclaimed himself their constitutional King".

He then stated that, apparently, some Indian chiefs acknowledged his authority while they were under the effects of generous quantities of liquor.

Besides, this diplomat informed that when Tounens was in Valparaíso, totally bankrupt, he offered to send him back to France but Tounens turned down his ticket because "I did not address him as Prince".

Shortly after returning to France Orllie Antoine published a book in Paris telling all about his experiences as King. He stated that France could have had extraordinary benefits in the reign he had founded.

In any case, he ended up in prison for not paying his debts.

The King of Patagonia was a Mason, and he suffered another drawback when Pope Pius IX excommunicated French Masonry in 1865. But Tounens begged forgiveness alleging his desire, as King of Araucania and Patagonia, to be reconciled with the Church.

The Pope wrote to the archbishop in Paris stating that "if these things proved to be true" then Tounens' request for pardon should be granted.

In 1869 Tounens again left for Argentina on board the French warship *d'Entrecasteaux*, with the tacit support of certain expansionist countrymen. He disembarked in San Antonio and went to Choele Choel, totally ignorant of the fact that the Indians there were belligerent. He was about to be slain when an *Araucano* recognised him and saved his life. He went on his way, to Chile, and was discovered in Araucania by Coronel Saavedra who had originally captured him ten years back. But this time the "King" was able to escape and managed to get to Bahía Blanca and then sailed to Buenos Aires. Some *Porteños* were delighted to share parties and all sorts of fun with Orllie Antoine, who then returned to Paris.

In 1874 he traveled for the third time to Argentina, stopping first in Buenos Aires and then going on to Bahía Blanca. In this case he was backed by the support of a banker, Jacob Michael, part of the press and some imperial chauvinists.

But he was recognized by Coronel Murga who sent him as a prisoner back to Buenos Aires and he was then deported to France.

Apparently, the banker's support was due to something that Orllie told him, in absolute confidence:

"that in the Andean Mountain Range, there are treasure mines; and that he would extract those treasures in no time".

In time, Orllie Antoine's fame was forgotten. He died a poor man, in a public hospital in Tourtoirac.

His successor to the throne, Achilles I (Gustave Achille Laviarde) never saw Patagonia, but he received a lot of money from investors who believed his promise about "making big business in the New France". This colony would, of course, be established in the realm founded by his noble predecessor, Orllie Antoine.

9.- AND WALES SHALL BE KING...

The Welsh thought they had reached the Promised Land – "We have found a better land in a far-off region down South" – They worked hard and suffered all sorts of hardships - Their valuable support in the demarcation of limits with Chile – They settled in Chubut

After centuries of having been oppressed in their own country, discriminated in their habits, beliefs and language after the annexing to England in 1536, thousands of Welsh believed that exile could bring them back some of their lost identity. Besides, they were used to hard labor in coal mines back home, to living in mean shacks in sordid villages, so...what could they lose?

In the 1860s, in contempt of the British Empire (that had consolidated its dominion over Wales after stifling the uprising led by national leader Owen Glendower), more than two hundred thousand Welsh emigrated to different destinations: the U.S.A., Canada, Australia, Brazil and...Patagonia.

Traditionalists by nature and fervent Christians when the English were still heathen, the Welsh built their much revered Saint David Cathedral, in 1100. They also developed a rich and expressive literature that enriched their language. Wherever they went, they always pursued the same goal: to be able to speak their language exclusively; they believed it was the basis of their identity. So, losing their language would mean losing their true self.

And in Great Britain they were forced to express themselves in English, a language they despised and felt alien to their traditions, their songs and poetry, their idiosyncrasy.

They wanted to profess their religion and lead their lives under the inspiration of the Bible. Therefore, more than homesickness for what they left behind, their hearts filled with hope in this Promised Land, where they would be fully and completely Welsh, both in speech and in spirit. At last...

Towards Patagonia

Why choose Patagonia?

Who knows...

The first negotiation was carried out by a sailor, Love Jones-Parry, Baron of Madryn, and a young typographer called Lewis Jones, in a formal meeting with Minister Rawson, during Mitre´s presidency. As neither of these men spoke Spanish, they needed an interpreter. We can imagine the translator´s surprise at having to transmit to the Minister the intention of the new immigrants, which was no other than founding a Welsh nation within Argentina.

Very cleverly, Rawson did nothing to discourage this rather naïve desire. His unspoken thoughts were maybe that time would bring about the inevitable. And meanwhile he would attract immigrants to populate a region that for over three hundred and fifty years had expelled them.

The envoys went back home and described what they thought they had seen, although they hadn´t carried out any proper survey of the territory, just what they managed to see from the ship´s deck. Lewis Jones reported having seen

> "low hills with not a living soul. The grass is shoulder-high and the apples, cherries and plums are so plentiful that the river just carries them away. There are thousands of cows with their calves and big flocks of red sheep. There is also a nearby market where the women could sell butter."

For these hill people, the idea of the "flat lands" suggested prairies where things grow naturally, with no effort involved.

Were these delirious ideas of Lewis Jones simply a way of convincing himself that he was on the right path? Or was it his fantasy, that mistook myth for reality?

The fact is that yearning for freedom needs a certain amount of dreams and illusion to make it come true. And besides, weren´t the mythical *Trapalanda* and the *Ciudad de los Césares* what kept alive the interest in the still undiscovered Patagonia?

The Welsh writer Horwell Jones pointed out that his countrymen, like most hill people, were reluctant to change, lacking in flexibility and puritans where religion was concerned.

> "Crude necessity has turned them into crafty, practical men, but, being Celts they have the fortune –or is it the curse?- of having a

vivid imagination. Behind the wise mask of every man there hides a guileless dreamer..."

Maybe, when leaving Liverpool on the 28th of May of 1865, they had a vision, that they were heading for the Promised Land. Then, all together, with hearts filled with hope, they sang a hymn:

> *We have found a better land*
> *In a far off region in the South,*
> *In Patagonia.*
> *There we shall live in peace*
> *Without fear of traitors nor swords*
> *And there Wales shall be King:*
> *Hallowed be the Lord.*

Unfortunately, they disembarked in winter on the 28th of July. The one hundred and fifty one Welsh -including women and children- were met by cold rain and a strong gale. During the non-stop voyage two babies were born and another four died.

Lewis Jones and Eldwin C. Roberts (Welsh resident in the U.S.A. and fervent defender of establishing a colony) were there to greet them, the flag with the red dragon flying in the wind.

Three days after their arrival, the *Mimosa* left port. It must have been with a somber heart that the newcomers watched the sails disappearing on the horizon.

Women and children sought shelter in some wooden shacks and the men lived in caves on the coast. There was no water to be found and, faced with this God-forsaken place, they finally decided to leave, heading for the valley of the river Chubut.

The women went by sea on a barge called *Mary Helen*. For days they were at the mercy of a violent storm that juggled the ship like a helpless toy. The cold was unbearable and very soon they had finished the meager supply of food and water.

The men crossed the desert on foot, guided by Eldwin Roberts. Cold, hunger and thirst were their permanent companions. On the way they were forced to kill a *carancho* (local bird of prey) and suck its blood. Others got sick after drinking salt water. And there was still another nightmare, the constant fear of an Indian attack.

After four days of marching under these terrible conditions, old Mr. William Roberts improvised a cot under a bush and announced to all that he was staying there to die. The others went on their way and the next day, at dawn, they reached the river banks. They avidly drank water once and again and some went back to look for Roberts who, apparently, when he had quenched his thirst decided to go on living.

Settling down

The Welsh are a people of action. They lost no time in establishing the foundation of their first village. They built huts with adobe, and fishing and hunting provided them with the basic food supply.

The sermon of the first religious service alluded symbolically to "Israel in the desert".

On the 15th of September Commander Julián Murga granted the Welsh settlers possession of those lands, and that deed marked the origin of the town of Rawson. Figuring in its foundation deeds is the following statement:

> "This will be in benefit of all the country in general. After which, and once the Argentine flag has been hoisted and saluted by the firing of guns as a sign of respect and obedience to the Argentine Nation it represents, the Colony of the Country of Wales is established".

Signing the Act were Julián Murga, the land surveyor Julio V. Díaz –who measured and marked plots of land for five hundred families- and Lewis Jones.

W. H. Hughes was of the opinion that "the hoisting of the Argentine flag, that day, was a mortal blow" to the idea of building a Welsh Nation. Nevertheless, not one of those present had a single word of complaint.

But there were difficult times ahead.

Sowing yielded no positive results, cattle scattered in search of water and pastures, and soon the villagers were obliged to adopt food rationing.

The time came when they blamed Lewis Jones for having lied to them as regards the "bountiful" lands where they would create another Wales.

Jones transferred his authority to William Davies and both traveled to

Buenos Aires to ask for help. As a gesture of good will, both the Argentine Government and the English subjects co-operated with the suffering settlers and sent them supplies.

But the problem was not only the hostile land and the tough climate. There was yet another difficulty and that is that the Welsh were a people accustomed to working in mines. They were not very good at farming, and therefore they had to face one failure after another. Lots of them gave up and left the colony. One of the deserters was the physician who had traveled with them from Liverpool.

A delegate of the Government of Buenos Aires and the secretary of the British Embassy traveled to the colony on board the English ship *Triton*. They checked that the Argentine government had actually sent the help that had been promised, and that the Welsh stayed on by their own decision.

The newcomers helped the settlers in different ways. The doctor on board treated the sick and translated from Latin to English the labels on the medicines the Welsh doctor had left them so they could be used in the future. The captain provided boots to whoever needed them, and the crew collected money which was donated to the settlers to buy woolen materials. They were really most surprised at the kindness shown by the English, and seven of the settlers chose to return to England on board the *Triton*. Others had already left for Choele-Choel to found another colony, and others did the same in Santa Fe, Río Negro or Patagones.

Soon after the *Triton* left those shores, the *Tehuelche* Indians set up camp near the Welsh colony and began a friendly relationship with the settlers, which was altogether very positive because the natives taught them many useful things. For example, they showed them how to handle cattle, how to ride and go hunting, apart from other tips such as the proper use of the *boleadoras*. They also provided them with *guanaco* and ostrich meat which they exchanged for some tasty Welsh bread, butter and cooked meat.

But time went by and things didn´t improve. Agriculture was still a tremendous failure, and eventually, when they again had to face a scarcity of food and basic supplies they became demoralized and decided to quit. Roberts and Davies were appointed to represent the settlers and traveled to Buenos Aires to request the grant of new lands, preferably in the province of Santa Fe. This request was denied but more help was promised instead.

On their return they were joined by Lewis Jones who had stayed in

Buenos Aires working at the Mulhalls' printing shop.

On reaching Madryn they found the settlers waiting for the ship, all ready to leave; they had abandoned the valley. Lewis Jones did everything in his power to try and convince them to stay on; he urged them not to leave their land, and to try and fulfil their dream of becoming a Welsh nation. Some were persuaded to stay but seven families chose the ship that would take them home.

Those who returned to the colony received a tremendous blow: they discovered most of the houses had been burnt down. Apparently that was *Tehuelche* work. After all they had done to help the Welsh, the natives resented their leaving and, out of spite, started the fire.

The Welsh resignedly tried to start all over again, but a drought threatened their crops. Only this time, fortunately, luck seemed to be on their side.

Rachel Jones and her husband, Aaron Jenkins, were forlornly going over the sown lands when suddenly the wife realized the river ran on a level higher than the land. Without a moment's hesitation, they opened a furrow and, enthralled, watched the water flowing onto the crops.

This of course caused a commotion in the community, suddenly aware that this system of irrigation was the solution to the drought problem.

In 1874 a new group of Welsh immigrants arrived, from the United States. Some of them were expert farmers and were gradually able to modernize the agricultural techniques.

A result of this new commercial activity was the first cereal shipment.

The town of Gaiman was founded in 1875 (Gaiman means grinding stone in *Tehuelche* language). A census carried out in 1878 revealed the following facts: living in the colony were seven hundred and fifty-nine inhabitants; there were forty-eight births registered; livestock amounted to two thousand four hundred head of cattle, seven hundred horses, three thousand fowl and eight hundred and fifty-nine sheep; cultivated fields were fifteen thousand hectares. Two mills were built a couple of years later.

Perseverance, imagination and hard work seemed to have changed the destiny of the Welsh colony which had, in the beginning, seemed doomed to failure just like the attempts of Sarmiento de Gamboa, Floridablanca, Deseado and so many others...

Thanks to the newly discovered irrigation system, the lower valley of the

Chubut river became the most important agricultural region. Cereal production allowed for an increase in trading with Buenos Aires and even Liverpool.

Population increased and so did the number of small landowners, who gradually formed a commercial guild; its management was entrusted to the religious leaders, who not only looked after the spiritual welfare of the community but were also tough men who worked on a par with the settlers.

Municipal authorities were democratically chosen. Progress was slow but steady. Soon the Welsh colony became self-sufficient in varied food produce and agricultural commodities.

Education and tradition

They published a newspaper and built a school. Even though the only book in Welsh was the Bible, that was how they managed to preserve their native tongue throughout time.

The writer H. Davies underlined the fact that a pupil of that first school named Eluned Morgan (daughter of Lewis Jones) wrote four books in the purest and most beautiful Welsh prose ever known.

> *"The main objective, that is preserving the Welsh language and style of life, had been achieved. Ties with the language were strong enough not only to make Indian children (orphans or abandoned children that the Welsh took under their care) become Welsh speaking people, but also to oblige Spanish speaking men marrying Welsh girls to learn it.*
>
> *In 1877 there were three Welsh schools; in 1888 the first national school was established; the Argentine government, anxious for children to learn something about the country, published five text books in Welsh. Even though the ultimate aim was to teach them Spanish, few governments have employed such an intelligent system..."*

On the other hand, Nicanor Larrain wrote:

> *"The Welsh strongly resist mixing with the "criollo" population, not even by way of the language, which they ignore and show no interest in learning; they even keep their costumes intact.*
>
> *The Welsh are as honest as they are hard working people; they are*

*also cultured; a genteel, slight curtsy bending both knees is the
ladies' way of greeting"*

And then he went on to say that there were seven Protestant churches
including Methodist, Baptist and Independent which

*"became famous thanks to Oliver Cromwell; I visited the latter and
found it most philharmonic; in fact, all their ceremonies are
celebrated singing".*

In December of 1878, during a meeting of Welsh leaders held in Gaiman,
David Lloyd Jones was elected judge and this is what he stated in his speech:

*"If we cannot get a local set of laws for education, then I would
rather we threw the government's money into the river"*

What really mattered was

*"that education be given in Welsh. But I also want every child to be
able to express himself both in Welsh and in Spanish, that way he
will be in a position to show the English contempt. God forbid that
we forget our language, but may He not want us to sacrifice
knowledge in the name of language".*

No matter how hard the Welsh worked on their project, they always
needed –and usually received- all the help the government could give them.
During Sarmiento's presidency they were even offered better lands which the
colonists rejected because they were stubbornly intent on creating the Welsh
nation there where they had built their churches.

Another major event was the construction of the Puerto Madryn – Trelew
railway, for which more than four hundred and fifty Welsh people came over
from Great Britain on board the *Vesta*.

On the 28th of May of 1885 coronel Luis Jorge Fontana was appointed
Governor of Chubut. He fostered a period of progress for the Welsh colony,
which extended beyond Gaiman towards the inner part of the territory. He
created the Compañía de Rifleros de Chubut with thirty initial volunteers, and
on the 14th of October they traveled West, coasting both shores of the river
Chubut and carrying out very detailed surveys of the rivers Genoa, Tecka,
Senguer and of the lakes Musters and Calhué Huapi, in Comodoro Rivadavia
and other regions. And then they reached the valleys next to the Andean
range ...and were immediately seduced by their breathtaking beauty.

With a remarkable show of tact, Fontana founded the colony on the 16th of

October (in memory of the date when the law 1884 –by which Patagonia was divided into Territorios Nacionales- was sanctioned) and managed to have a league allotted to each member of this expedition. Fifty leagues of land were distributed; these were measured by the Welsh engineer Llwyd Ap Iwan – murdered some years later by the North American gangster Willie Wilson-, and granted to the families who were to settle in the new colony: Austin, Thomas, Hopkins, Williams, Jones, Underwood, Davies, Warton, Howell, Freeman, Winn, Evans, Roberts, among others. In that colony there were thirty-nine Welsh, five Argentines, two North Americans, two English and two Germans.

Luis Jorge Fontana was described by Lewis Jones as a "lucid and affable man". He didn´t keep a plot of land for himself; his only interest was in looking after the colonists´ welfare and security, and seeing that all the terms that were agreed upon with the authorities were duly observed. Coronel Fontana had a very high opinion of the Welsh community; above all he respected their idealism and hard-working disposition. He found their customs most intriguing, specially when they rode on horseback wearing extravagant getups such as *"top hats, morning coats, quillangos, ponchos, belts made out of boleadoras, sabers and rifles"*

Among the Welshmen that formed part of the Compañía de Rifleros was John Daniel Evans, a scout who worked in close collaboration with Fontana. Evans had reached Argentina on board the *Mimosa* with his family, when he was three years old. All his life had been a sequence of hardships, sacrifice and very few gratifying moments. As a kid he made friends with the son of the Indian chief Wisel, who taught him to how to ride and hunt, and to roam through the plains and deserts just like a native. But most surprising of all was that this same *Tehuelche* gave John serious advice as to how it suited him to leave these barren lands and go West where he would find green pastures, trees, *cimarrón* (unclaimed) animals , gold, snow and lakes.

It finally turned out that way. But before escorting Fontana on a scouting expedition he decided to go and look for some gold.

The tragic episode he went through is still present in the minds and memories of the townspeople as one of the most terrible events in Welsh history.

John Evans and his Expedition

John Evans had organized an expedition to escort captain Richards, an Australian who had come to these lands in the hope of finding gold. The group consisted initially of seven men, but three deserted leaving Evans, John Parry, John Hughes and Richard David to set forth on this adventurous quest. They moved westwards, and when camping at the confluence of the rivers Lepa and Chubut, they were approached by two *Araucanos* of the *Foyel* tribe; they invited the four men to accompany them to the Indian camp in Súnica, right next to the Cordillera. They were so insistent that Evans became suspicious, specially when he saw one of the Indians galloping at full speed towards the camp while the other two tried to divert their attention.

So, the Welshmen finally decided to go on their way. They traveled day and night stopping only for a change of horses. They were careful to ride only on stony ground or in the river bed so as not to leave any traces. But Parry and Hughes were worn out and, when the moon came out, they took a rest next to a well. Unfortunately the well was dry.

They had been riding for several days and were so exhausted that occasionally one of them would fall off the horse. Then they would stop just to drink some coffee. Whenever one of them was too tired to go on, the others would tie him with a lasso to the saddle to avoid his falling off the horse.

They were always on the lookout in case they were being followed by the Indians. But, after riding for some time they saw nothing suspicious and presumed they had lost their trail. They cooked some wild hares for lunch and then slept soundly, before resuming their ride towards Las Plumas.

When they were crossing the dry bed of a lagoon, under a blazing sun, they suddenly heard what Evans described as "some terrible yelling and shouting that froze the blood in our veins. It was the savages´ battle cry". They were unaware that, during all their ride the Indians had followed them along the river bed. That way they left no telltale clouds of dust.

The men were taken by surprise and, before they were able to recover their wits they were surrounded by thirty fierce looking natives. Evans saw David falling to the ground, wounded by a spear. He also saw how his other two friends were attacked although they were still in their saddles.

In later reports, Evans told how he spurred his horse on and, with an impetuous jump, managed to break up the circle the Indians had formed around them. The moment the horse lurched forward, an Indian grasped his spear and attempted to thrust it at him. But Evans struck him a nasty blow and diverted the spear. Then he escaped at a full gallop, the horde of Indians behind him screaming wildly.

The natives tried to get at Evans's horse with *boleadoras* while he got hold of his gun. He reached the edge of a ditch about four meters deep and his *malacara* (local breed of horses) jumped across to the other side. After that, rider and horse, hot, tired and sweating, advancing at a slow pace half hidden by some shrubs, managed to get away from the Indians. They headed for the valley. But they had two full days and one night of traveling ahead of them. At a slow pace, sometimes trotting, Evans took detours, always on the alert, afraid of an ambush. Above all, he was scared that the wounded hoofs of his *malacara* could leave give-away blood trails.

He was so paranoid that when he saw a rider at a distance he felt paralyzed with fear. He didn't know whether to hide, or run...until the other man approached, and Evans, overjoyed, recognized one of the colonists from the valley.

That night, when Evans was giving them all the details of his dramatic experience, the men were impressed and perplexed by the attitude of the aggressors. Nobody expected such a show of cruelty. But, on the other hand, it was common knowledge that when it came to *Foyel* and its *Araucanos* "whatever they fixed their gaze upon became a target for their spears"

Upon his arrival a search squad was organized. It was led by Lewis Jones, who was convinced that the Welsh attacked by the Indians were not dead, just held captive in the Indian camp.

They marched for eight long days. The sight of *caranchos* flying in circles over the area where the attack had taken place filled them with a sense of foreboding.

After that, the dead bodies were quite easy to find... there were the three young men, mutilated. Their hearts had been wrenched from their bodies. They were castrated, their genitals in their mouths in an advanced stage of decay.

They never really recovered from the shock. With tremendous effort they managed to bury the bodies. With a trembling voice Lewis Jones said a prayer in the Anglican church style, and then they all sang a Welsh hymn, their sad voices carrying over these desolate lands. Since then this place is called Valle de los Mártires.

When the horse belonging to Evans –the legendary *malacara*- died, he buried it and placed a stone where he engraved this epitaph:

> "*Here lie the remains of my horse El Malacara, who saved my life during the Indian attack in the Valle de los Mártires on the 4ᵗʰ /3 / 84, on my return from the Cordillera*".

John Evans´s reports proved to be most useful for the country. He affirmed having reached the Andes without seeing any flags which prompted Coronel Luis Jorge Fontana to organize his Rifle squad and march westward to plant the Argentine flag at the foot of the Cordillera and start a new colony.

The flood

The year 1899 will be remembered as one of the most dramatic in the history of the Welsh colony, on account of the flood that destroyed many years of hard work. Standing at the top of the hills, three thousand troubled settlers watched the river overflowing, the water quickly invading the sown fields and the dwellings, drowning the cattle, leaving sand deposited in the irrigation ditches.

Like a macabre turn of the screw, the water which had made progress possible was now the cause of its destruction.

Thanks to some riders who alerted them about the danger that was in store for them, they were at least able to save their lives. They escaped to the hills before the flood caught up with them.

What a poignant scene, thousands of eyes watching their belongings being destroyed! Heartbroken people huddling together seeking comfort from one another...Children crying in the arms of helpless mothers.

Eluned Morgan wrote:

> "*The home of my youth was just a mound of rubble, and we, just fugitives on the hills without shelter nor roof over our heads, ...It seemed like heaven had given its back to the place that used to be so flourishing, the first settlers´ Canaan*".

She also stressed how painful it was for a people who were so traditionalist to lose the "thousand family relics" which were maybe more important than all the material losses.

This is what H. Davies wrote about the attitude shown by the Welsh when faced with disaster:

> *"Destruction was so complete that a Canadian representative urged them to abandon the project and emigrate to his country. Some two hundred were taken to Winnipeg in 1902, but the rest were so fond of the valley that they preferred to stay and work towards the reconstruction of their colony. Wales was both touched and concerned by this turn of events. In 1911 it sent a group –the last- of one hundred and twenty colonists. But the reconstruction of the settlement was such a demanding feat that even a large number of Argentine workers came to help. And they stayed on. That was the first time that the solid Welsh front was broken by Spanish speaking men".*

Once more the Welsh were able to overcome an ill-fated event. They started all over again, peacefully working towards their ideals, with the spirit of heroic determination that had always characterized them.

They finally triumphed over ruthless nature and its creatures: crude winters, the arid desert and the ceaseless wind...

Wales and the Indians

Few communities have been so understanding and caring of the Indians as the Welsh. Eluned Morgan was full of sympathy for the natives. And she explained her point of view:

> *"The few hundred Indians that had managed to escape from the soldiers and took shelter in the mountains were so crazy with fear, their passions seized by demons to such an extent that only one overwhelming desire filled their hearts: to avenge the blood of their loved ones. What Welsh person could ever blame them?"*

And as for Lewis Jones, he writes in his book that in a letter written to the government, the Welsh revealed that they had:

> *"received many favors from these Indians ever since the settlement*

was founded, and that we have hardly ever had anything to fear from the fact of us being neighbors. In truth, the Indians were like a wall that gave us protection and defense. We believe that, in the same way as their trading was very useful to us, the existence of small groups of Indians nearby would always be a help when it came to establishing new colonies".

They also asked the government to be "kind and helpful to them".

The Welsh colony had always been vulnerable to the attack of the natives, and yet they had managed to lead a peaceful coexistence. The lands where they established the colony were *Tehuelche* territory, and very far from Carmen de Patagones.

If by any chance they had needed help, it wouldn´t have arrived on time. The Indians were quite aware of that.

That fact was also mentioned by the journalist Gorraiz Beloqui when referring to the *Araucanos*, who were not as peaceful or considerate as the Tehuelches, and had installed their camp in Choele-Choel. This tribe devastated all the province of Buenos Aires with systematic *malones* (Indian raids). If they had wanted to attack the Welsh colony they could have done so with very little effort.

But the fact is that the Welsh never suffered an attack except for that outrageous episode of the young gold seekers, and in that case it was provoked specifically by the Indian chief Foyel. That was also taken into account by the Welsh.

The Welsh community´s gradual incorporation into Argentine society was altogether positive, specially when it came to reaffirming national sovereignty in the boundaries problem with Chile: their wish to live by the Argentine flag expressed in the plebiscite of 1902 strongly supported our national claim.

Roca, during a visit to the colony in 1899, acknowledged that

"you have fought not only against this rough, cruel nature but also against a much more powerful enemy which is isolation and loneliness. Just for that you deserve the gratitude of our nation".

10.- GEORGE CHAWORTH MUSTERS – THE VOYAGE

He was named the Marco Polo of Patagonia – He went through a very demanding training in order to join the Tehuelches on their long journey – His close relationship with the natives – William Andrew and his adventures

> *"I had read the delightful work of Mr. Darwin about South America, and Fitz Roy´s remarkable account of the Beagle´s voyage; since then I always had a strong desire to explore the scarcely known interior of the country".*

These words were written by George Chaworth Musters.

Musters was an officer of the Royal Navy. He came from an upper-class family where most men belonged to the Navy. His father died when he was a year old and his mother when he was three. He was raised by some uncles; one of them was Robert Hammond, who had traveled with Fitz Roy on the voyage aboard the *Beagle*.

But in this case, Musters the seaman had a secret desire which was not in keeping with his profession. What he wanted was to travel overland. Up to that moment, only the *Tehuelches* had done it. He was the first white man to carry out this feat and that is why he was nicknamed "the Marco Polo of Patagonia".

At the time he was twenty-seven years old and retired from the Navy. His true vocation was exploring and adventurous living. What enhanced his desire to carry out this plan were all the stories about the *Tehuelches´* personality and the tales about the delightful entertainment of *guanaco* hunting.

So, he proceeded to train himself for this task. He spoke Spanish, as did the *Tehuelches*, and the fact that they could speak the same language made him feel confident that he could "safely cross the country in the company of some errant Indian parties".

Mc Dean, an acquaintance of his, and a resident of Malvinas gave him a letter of introduction addressed to Captain Luis Piedra Buena, whom he considered

> *"an intelligent Argentine very well-known in Stanley, owner of a*

schooner which he used to exploit the seal-fishing industry along the coast, and who also owns a factory in the Isla del Medio (Pavón) on the Santa Cruz river."

Previous arrangements

In 1869 Musters was in Punta Arenas, a place he considered "incredibly gloomy from the social point of view". When he discovered that he wouldn't be able to join any Indian group he decided to leave Punta Arenas anyway and traveled with an army patrol in search of deserters. Twelve days later he reached the island of Pavón and was greeted by Mr.Clarke who was in charge of Piedra Buena´s establishment.

By sheer chance, it turned out that the famous Indian chiefs Orkeke and Casimiro were camping in the neighborhood. So, during the winter Musters, who was clever and very much of a diplomat, became friendly with the *Tehuelches*. In the meantime he continued to train in hunting and short travels. Casimiro approved of Musters´ joining the caravan and persuaded Orkeke in the same sense. According to Musters, at the beginning Orkeke "was reluctant to allow the Englishman to join his party" As an excuse he referred to rough traveling, the length of the journey, the risk of some occasional battle, etc.

Musters was very impressed by Orkeke and his "grave, solemn carriage". "Six feet tall and well-built, nobody would have guessed this man was already in his sixties; and when he jumped onto his barebacked horse or led the hunting party, he went about it like a young man".

> *"He wore clean clothes and was tidy in his personal care. But, nevertheless, like all Indians, he was a victim of parasites(...) One night he woke me up to join him in a smoke and, after a long silence, he emerged from his deep thoughts and said: !Musters, lice never sleep!"*

The two Indian chiefs had opposite personalities. Orkeke was reflective and wise; on the other hand, Casimiro was unpredictable, temperamental and partial to *aguardiente* (a type of liquor). In the meantime Musters proved that, besides looking out for himself and his horse, he was also capable of acquiring Indian customs. He did like them: slept outdoors covered only by a *guanaco* hide, ate with them, resisted physical effort…

The adventure begins

He was allowed to join the caravan and, together with sixty natives of different ages –including women and children- departed in August of 1869. The itinerary was made out according to the stopping places where they would find water, firewood and grass. The first stop would be in Rio Chico, then they would continue on their way up to Geylum and they calculated reaching Patagones (Rio Negro) in March of the following year.

The Indians moved around with ease; no matter how harsh the climate or how rough the physical conditions, nothing seemed to daunt them. But they were a quarrelsome bunch, and, in fact, more than half the men died in some brawl. During the journey they also suffered an epidemic which killed many women and children.

During their long march they encountered many Indian camps and Musters never let pass an opportunity of talking at length with the chiefs and old men of the tribe. He was a unique case, the first white man who lived like one of them, taking part in their customs, their beliefs, their ceremonies, and who followed the rules of the Indian community.

He ate their food and shared many hunting parties. He was always present at their celebrations and witnessed their fights and quarrels.

He was also a good listener and sympathetic with the Indian cause. A brother of Chief Quintihual confided to Musters his fear concerning the future of his race. He complained about the treatment they got from the "Spanish", that is "the Chileans and the Argentines that invaded their lands". Of course they would fight to protect their tribe and their lands, but, even so, the future seemed anything but promising.

Although Musters had met many Indians for whom he felt admiration and respect he had a special relationship with chief Hinchel, whom he considered the best *Tehuelche*. He described him as:

> *"sincere and honest, generous, a man of temperance and totally apt for his function as chieftain. He is an expert at all the Indian tasks, whether it is breaking in a horse, or making a saddle or carving a*

silver necklace. If it hadn't been for his only vice, gambling, he would no doubt have been the richest and most powerful Indian chief. Everybody respected him."

He also told how one evening, when all the men were sitting round the fire talking, a messenger interrupted their conversation. There was blood on his face and he gesticulated wildly. Obviously he was drunk, and very excitedly started to tell how the previous night their party had encountered another group of natives that carried *aguardiente*. That of course led to an orgy and then a drunken brawl that resulted in one man being slaughtered. They just dumped him outside the tent, literally threw him to the dogs that devoured his dead body while the natives continued drinking. One of the victim's companions fled to see his chief, Saiyhueque and told him what had happened. Saiyhueque promptly sent a group of twenty-five warriors to demand payment for the death they had caused.

The indians' refusal led to a battle in which five men of Musters' group were seriously wounded. None died, though, and one of them managed to get away after killing four of Saiyhueque's men.

Musters' comments regarding this bloody event:

> *"The fact that six men fight against twenty-five may sound strange but, in my opinion, the people of Quintuhual and Foyel are the bravest Indians to be found in southern America and deserve the proud title of "Indian warriors".*

Besides stressing on the fighting qualities of Foyel and his people, Musters also showed admiration for Margarita, the chief's daughter. Her main occupation was sewing. She owned no less than eighty mares, and had a *Tehuelche* girl at her service with the sole purpose of looking after her hair-do.

Musters, a keen observer

Musters wrote at length about the Indian tribes, their characteristics and behavior. He got to know them very well and his comments show he was an acute observer. The same goes for his descriptions of the Indian chiefs. As regards Saiyhueque, this is what he wrote:

"This Indian chief was fully conscious of his high rank and power; his round, jovial face, with skin a shade darker than that of his subjects inherited from his tehuelche mother, showed a sly cunning; he laughed frequently, always with a hint of mockery. He held his head high and from his regal stance looked down at Casimiro whom he despised because of his drunkenness; obviously, he considered himself –quite rightly- superior to all other Indian chiefs".

Another time, Musters commented that the natives

"were fully conscious of the advantages of peacetime; on the other hand, they all –and most especially the araucanos- strongly resisted foreign usurpers. Traditions evolving from their past history had driven them to hate the mere mention of the word Spanish or Christian."

He also told how

"many peacemaking efforts carried out by government authorities had failed due to the devious dealings of certain unscrupulous agents who profited by stealing the supplies that were destined for the Indians ".

Musters took part in the natives' hunting parties and sorties:

"One day I went on an excursion with the children. We pulled up spinach and looted the nests of wild ducks and geese; we returned with our arms laden with these goods and that evening we cooked a tehuelche stew with ostrich grease, eggs and spinach".

He also went fishing, but except for Casimiro, the Indians didn't eat fish.

Musters described special methods used by the Indians to cook ostriches or a type of *peludo* (*piches*): they empty the animal's belly, fill the cavity with very hot stones and then sew it up. That way it takes less time to cook and the meat is juicier.

His diary was looked upon by the Indians with a mixture of suspicion and curiosity. This moved Musters to consider:

"If any "ignorant" Indian were to suspect that he would one day figure in print, one could logically presume that he would rather proceed to destroy the author himself instead of waiting to destroy the book".

The Indians firmly believed in the existence of an unknown tribe or an enchanted city that remained undiscovered. This legend originated many different stories.

As regards the Indians´ commercial trading, Musters says they used to visit the Welsh colonies in Chubut, because "it was safer and more pleasant to deal with the honest Welsh settlers than with the *cristianos* of Rio Negro". They were most impressed by the size and quality of the home-made bread, which they exchanged for half a *guanaco*.

Chief Jackechan not only appreciated the quality of their bread, he also liked the Welsh because of their kindness: they used to "give shelter to the Indian when he was under the effect of aguardiente; quite the opposite to the people of Rio Negro (Patagones) who would steal his clothes and all his belongings".

The Indian chief had met Lewis Jones and always carried his picture around. Jones had revealed the name of the Queen of England; chief Jackechan was most curious about her and wanted Musters to give him more information. Musters wrote: "I could see he was a very intelligent Indian; he spoke spanish, pampa and tehuelche fluently; our relationship soon developed into a bond of mutual friendship".

On one opportunity they celebrated parliament; Jackechan and other Indian chiefs were present and, according to Musters:

"...they all agreed to submit to Casimiro´s authority with the purpose of defending Patagones in case it should be invaded by Roque or Calfucurá (...) All those present acknowledged it was imperative to defend Patagones, because destruction of the colony would mean the end of a market where they could trade their hides, etc."

In Carmen de Patagones

When Musters reached Patagones he was impressed by this "modern" city which had, he calculated, around two thousand inhabitants.

> *"It is divided into four very distinct social classes: 1) the descendants of the first Spanish settlers; 2) the more recent foreign immigrants; 3) the African ex-slaves 4) The Argentine prisoners."*

He was intrigued by the descendants of the Spaniards, or *maragatos,* who kept to themselves in a close circle that excluded all "outsiders". They only married among themselves and practically formed one sole, large family.

> *"The men stand out for their kindness and courteous hospitality, while the ladies show a beauty and graciousness of manner that could easily match those of the old Spain or other Argentine provinces".*

He also pointed out their zeal in the practice of their religion.

And as for the foreigners, they were "a heterogeneous group of people of different nationalities, mostly Italians and Spanish Basques. There are also quite a few French, English, Welsh, Swiss and Germans."

In his opinion, the Africans were a "fine and long-suffering race" which had decreased enormously due to the "recruitment for the Army and to the small-pox".

Regarding the prisoners, he remarked that Patagones lacked the strict discipline that characterized the penal colony in Punta Arenas, and the city was full of "people who had deserted from the Army, thieves and criminals of all types sent over from Buenos Aires". They weren't likely to escape, because by sea it was impossible and by land they would surely be killed by the Indians. So they mingled with the other townspeople and had no restrictions whatsoever. The result was, of course, that they resorted to thieving (stealing horses mostly) and received no punishment for it. As regards the murder cases, he wrote:

> *"In the rare cases where the criminals are discovered, it means they are simply sent back to Buenos Aires to be judged in a court of law; this, in turn, results in a sentence by which they are once again deported to Rio Negro. It has been said that a certain Ruiz had come and gone four times to Buenos Aires (...) and that he openly*

boasted about killing someone whenever he wanted a free trip".
An employee working under the Commanding Officer´s orders was also a convict charged with manslaughter.

"My friend don Pablo (Piedra Buena, brother of Luis) was attacked one evening next to his home, but luckily he was able to get away unharmed. Murders happen all the time and everybody must bear arms of some sort in self-defense".

Of course, as Musters ironically put it, the unprotected inhabitants of Patagones "can brag about having an excellent, new cemetery up north", whereas the old cemetery that lies in the East, "shows coffins appearing through the sand, and in some cases they are uncovered; skulls and bones strewn on the ground, and even a cat can be seen jumping in and out of a coffin".

Musters admired the working capacity of the settlers as well: "the farms outlying towards the West, and the delightful looking islands along the river towards the South"; the most outstanding was the island where don Benito Crespo had his vineyard where he produced –and hoped to export- "a wine called *chacoli*, which has the flavor of the muscatel and the fragrance of *moselle*; it is a pure, light wine…"

Another important establishment was the salting factory owned by don Luis Aguirre, who "exported large quantities of hides and tallow to England".

The yield was good. Wheat could be sown and harvested year after year on the same land. Potatoes were large and of very good quality. Musters advised young, enthusiastic people who had saved some cash and weren´t afraid of hard work "to buy lands –that could be got at reasonable prices- and cultivate them". "The climate is pleasant and healthful and one good crop almost covers the cost of installing a medium-sized establishment".

The "rations" policy

Musters also commented on his meeting with Commander Murga, who was most intrigued about his relationship with the Indians. Realizing that Murga felt uneasy and perplexed, Musters hastened to assure him that his familiarity was that of "a guest and friend". The commander wasn´t altogether convinced. He looked over the chiefs´s requests and curtly assured him that they would receive the rations assigned to them.

The "rations" had been granted by Juan Manuel de Rosas as a way of guaranteeing "peaceful trading with the Indians". To that end, he provided them with supplies and military wages. But not all the natives accepted "donations". In fact, Rosas fought many battles against the *ranqueles* and the *araucanos* of the Andes, Rio Negro and Neuquén.

As a consequence of Rosas's policy there was relative peace for a number of years, but, as a counterpart, it fostered laziness and indolence in the natives. It also originated a new type of illegal trading, that of unscrupulous merchants who bought goods from the Indians for a few measly pennies. For example, they traded a pound of feathers that cost twenty pesos for a bottle of the cheapest liquor worth only ten cents.

As regards Casimiro, Commander Murga assured Musters that he would receive all that was due; as it had been several years that the Indian chief had refused to accept his ration, it now amounted to something like two hundred cows, one hundred mares, five hundred sheep and plenty of clothes and *yerba.*

> *"One can easily imagine that if Casimiro made good use of this visit he could become both a rich and powerful chieftain (...) On a previous visit he had left a considerable number of cows and sheep in the care of some peaceful natives, so that they could reproduce but, alas¡...only a small herd of sheep showed up; the rest had been gambled and lost by their guardians...."*

Musters also remembered witnessing the delivery of a thousand head of cattle to Cheoeque instead of the one thousand two hundred that were due, which made him think that the purveyors handled a very profitable business; the Indians let go of their belongings for a pittance and the animals returned to the purveyor's hands to be offered again as "ration".

Farewell

The time had come to say goodbye. He waited for the indians' return from Valcheta, where they had celebrated a long drunken orgy. "Of course Casimiro had set the example and the liquor had, as usual, caused the fighting to begin." Several natives died in this quarrel, some, like Cayuke or Waki, for whom Musters felt a special liking. Valcheta was guarded from the strong winds and served as a secret shelter for the natives. No white man knew the precise spot chosen by the Indians to install their tents.

"Groups of *Tehuelches* arrived during all that day; not knowing what to do, they followed me around wherever I went". Then came the *Araucanos* of the tribes of *Quintuhual* and *Foyel*. Quite the opposite to the humble *Tehuelches*, they were proud and haughty, showing no interest in anything they saw, lest somebody could think they were after some gift or present. They even refused to pay the boatman his fee for crossing them over, and when he complained they just pointed at him with a gun. The boatman, of course, looked the other side.

And as for Casimiro, he installed himself at the hotel and hired the garrison´s musicians to play while he had his lunch. During two full days anybody who wanted to go into the hotel could do so, and when he retired, he was usually completely drunk. According to Musters, Casimiro paid the cost of all this celebration with "almost half the value of the rations". Afterwards, and following the Englishman´s advice, Casimiro crossed the river and went to Sauce Blanco to watch over his people and his belongings.

When the Indians finally bade Musters farewell they urged him to return "as soon as possible". Musters gave them gifts: he presented Orkeke´s wife with an iron cooking-pot and a shawl, which she accepted deeply moved by his gesture. To the children he gave raisins, bread and candy, and a pack of cards to Hinchel´s son.

> *"Jackechan´s wife and daughter had always been very kind to me, so I took them to the store and told them to choose whatever they liked most; without a moment´s hesitation, the ladies chose two little bottles of perfume. I must add, by the way, that all this family was exceptionally clean both in person and in the clothes they wore; I promised I would travel in their tent if I should return to Patagonia, because I had the vague intention of traveling along the sea shore up to Chubut, and maybe to Santa Cruz.*
> *Jackechan´s son, the boy with fair hair and skin, offered to come with me to England and I accepted taking him under my charge; but he changed his mind when he found out there were no ostriches nor guanacos in the country we were going to".*

Musters and his significant experience

Few men have, like Musters, been able to have an inside knowledge of the Indians and their ways, their way of thinking and the patterns that have marked their history and determined their identity.

What Musters discovered, all he learnt and experienced in the heart of Patagonia and transcribed in the book "At Home with the Patagonians", was a revelation even to the Argentines.

Later explorers like Moyano, Lista and Moreno always had Musters´s work in mind as a personal reference and as a source of permanent "advice".

The Indians always had the highest opinion of this Englishman who had shown them affection and treated them with respect. Francisco P. Moreno remembered that once, when he was reading out loud certain paragraphs of that book, a *Tehuelche* woman named María, remarked: "Musters very cold. Very good he was, poor Musters".

Lista and Fontana also got favorable references of Musters from other natives who could clearly pronounce his name.

Fontana states that the experiences told by Musters in his chronicles urged the Welsh colonists to carry out deeper studies of Patagonia and to help in many reconnaissance tasks.

Some historians hint at the suspicion that Musters acted like an agent for the British Empire and that his discoveries in inner Patagonia were most useful for the capitals wanting to install English companies in lands suitable for agricultural projects. Nevertheless, the English had explored these lands for many years and owned a lot of information. If, on the other hand, this suspicion proved to be true, Musters acted involuntarily as a double agent. The question then is: who made better use of the information?

There is, though, a unanimous opinion that the urge that drove him to explore these strange territories was his love of adventure and a curious nature that had been most influenced by the narratives of Darwin and Fitz Roy.

William Andrew: an eccentric character

Another Englishman, William Andrew, a thirty-six-year-old wealthy and eccentric lawyer, was also attracted to the imposing landscape of Patagonia. Unlike Musters, he had no definite aim except to roam these lands wherever chance –and his horse- would take him. Neither did he have Musters´s particular urge to investigate and write down reports that would prove useful to other explorers. No geographical or ethnographic surveys. Even so, his journey turned out to be an unusual personal experience full of amusing anecdotes.

Andrew came from a prominent family of attorneys and worked in an important law firm in London. He lived in a beautiful house and was happily married to a very attractive young lady. We could say he led a good life until his wife died. He was grief-stricken and felt the need to get away from home, to leave his work behind and go someplace far away…

He sailed on his yacht in the company of some friends, with no particular port in mind. After several days sailing he thought it would be a good idea to stretch the voyage and get to South America. Maybe he had read the chronicles of English travelers, maybe he had even read the book Musters had published in London; the fact is, he reached Buenos Aires in 1881 and promptly took leave of his friends telling them that if he wasn´t back in three days they were to sail to Chile where they would meet. He did explain his motives: "he wanted to see guanacos and to hunt ostriches; and felt very curious about the ways and skills of the gauchos". He bade his friends farewell and said they would meet again in the Pacific, "crossing pampas and cordilleras".

His traveling companions were used to his eccentricities so they made no fuss about this and simply agreed to meet in the capital city of Chile.

E. Kincaid, an acquaintance of this English lawyer, explained to Nicanor Larrain the details concerning his decision: William Andrew traveled in the Ferrocarril del Sud down to Azul, where he was informed that he must travel yet further to see what he came to see. He continued his journey to Olavarría and then on to Bahía Blanca and finally reached Patagones. He was most surprised to see troops in action and was informed that it was an expedition led by General Villegas bound for the cordillera. He spoke to a high-ranking official and asked to be recruited. So, to everybody´s surprise, he joined the party.

According to E. Kincaid, William Andrew acquired *criollo* skills: he learnt to make halters, to handle the *maneador* and the lasso, throw the *boleadoras* to catch a *guanaco*, and even eat a *potro* (horse) steak which he found tastier than the customary beefsteak. He trained himself to ride under the rain and to endure many hours without eating or drinking; he also fought alongside the soldiers as one of them.

Once he rode up to General Roca and as night caught up with him he decided to camp out there. He always carried an inflatable rug with him which he used as a mattress, so he proceeded to prepare his "bed" and all the soldiers in the fort laughed at him. He paid no heed and just lay down trying to make the most of this rare moment of comfort. He christened his rug "doña Catalina", maybe in honor of someone he met in the past.

At dawn he left for Choele-Choel, and those who knew about his plan of going to Chile to meet his friends wondered when he would return. Nobody knew (least of all himself) what he would do next, or where he would go. He moved around aimlessly but that was no problem, just part of the fun.

At Choele-Choel he stopped to have dinner at a *fonda* belonging to a Spaniard who was married to a lovely *criolla* called Catalina. There he sat at table with other people he didn´t know and who seemed very intrigued as to the reason for his presence in these remote lands; he told many stories in a sort of spanglish which they all found very amusing.

When everybody was ready to retire, it seemed the few rooms available at the *fonda* (a sort of saloon) were already reserved. But the Englishman assured everyone he was perfectly fine: "No preocuparse por mí; dormir afuera con doña Catalina" (Don´t worry about me; I´ll sleep outside with doña Catalina). And he repeated, before leaving the inn: "Yo quiero mucho a Catalina y con ella duermo bien, así no preocuparse. Buenas noche" (I love doña Catalina very much and sleep very well with her, so don´t worry. Good night).

There was a tense silence. But then it all became clear when one of the men said that he watched Andrew while he arranged his rug and fondly pronounced her name while preparing for his sleep.

When Andrew was going to sleep he heard laughter coming from the inn. He guessed somebody had told a good joke…

He then traveled to Patagones. After riding for several ice-cold days, harassed by the wind, he got to the Río Negro river and crossed its frozen waters. When he reached the opposite side he saw a *rancho* (adobe hut) nearby and walked towards it, waving hello. Nobody answered, it seemed deserted. A shivering Andrew set the hut on fire and he warmed up and dried his clothes. Just when he was enjoying this warm moment he saw a *paisano* approaching, shouting and waving his arms. It was the owner of the rancho. Andrew tried to explain what had happened but the man was furious and screamed over the loss of his dwelling. The Englishman did his best to calm him and promised to make it up to him. The man stopped shouting, and ruefully accepted the payment Andrew offered him for the damage done.

He went over to Patagones and shared an *albergue* with an indian child who was being held captive. He was all set for his return when there came news that a Coronel Vintter was ready to march south. So he decided to join the expedition instead.

Nicanor Larrain, deputy to the Minister of Foreign Affairs, was in Deseado and about to board his ship when he suddenly saw the Englishman among Vintter´s troops. He watched William Andrew "cutting, sewing and putting on some gloves made of sheep skin that came up to his elbows", getting all set to leave for the cordillera.

The sergeant asked him:

- But then, you´re not going back?-

- Go back? Go back where?...

The Englishman finally took leave of the troop, camped out in Neuquén and then crossed over to Chile.

11.- YOUNG ARGENTINE EXPLORERS

Ramon Lista, Carlos Maria Moyano and Francisco Pascasio Moreno traveled all over the Patagonian territories carrying out surveys and research. Their dedication knew no bounds, no sacrifice was too great for them

The geopolitical concerns in the second half of the XIX Century were mainly: a) the controversy with Chile regarding the boundaries, and b) the need to populate Patagonia as a way of reinforcing sovereign rights by establishing military and civil settlements. All this demanded previous studies and reconnaissance tasks, and that is where the "young explorers" come into the picture. Their mission was to explore the vast Patagonian territories in order to carry out geographic assessments, and the necessary surveys that would allow for an adequate delimitation of boundaries and of the areas that were apt for colonization purposes.

Valentín Feilberg

In November 1873, the twenty-one-year-old Naval Lieutenant Valentín Feilberg together with four other men went to the Santa Cruz river. Their mission was to go up-river in a rowboat right to its source. After seventeen days of exhausting travel they reached the Valle del Misterio (named by Fitz Roy). On many opportunities they had to either tow the boat or carry it on their shoulders, so by the end of the day they were completely worn out and with sore hands. The landscape was arid and monotonous. Their surroundings were depressing. And when night caught up with them they couldn´t fight against the cold. Shivering, feeling dejected, they often wondered if they would be able to tame this impetuous river.

They decided to give it one more try, although their general state of fatigue and exhaustion made them doubt as to a positive outcome. They lay on the ground, resting and brooding over their failure, when suddenly Feilberg heard the familiar sound of waves breaking on the shore. He thought at first he was imagining things, that it was no more than an hallucination…

He gathered together the little strength he could muster and walked a few meters until the most incredible scenery appeared before his eyes: a vast, unending mass of water furrowed by huge icebergs. He thought he was looking at Lake Viedma, and actually gave it that name, although it was, in fact, the lake that perito Moreno called Lago Argentino some years later. Exploring the surroundings he discovered the river Leona and took possession of the place: planting an oar as if it were a mast, he flew the Argentine flag, at whose feet he left a message inside a bottle. The message was found by Moreno who made it known to the world, and christened the place Punta Feilberg.

Ramón Lista

Ramón Lista was another explorer who afforded valuable services to his country, although he sometimes incurred in impetuous actions that were severely criticized.

His studies dealt mainly with geography and natural sciences, subjects in which he specialized during his courses in Europe.

At the age of twenty-two, together with lieutenant Moyano, they explored the rivers Santa Cruz, Chico and Chalía, and a few months later, in 1878, the bay of San Julián.

In January of 1885 he led an expedition from Bahía Blanca to Deseado, and then Choele-Choel, Valcheta and the colony of Chubut. The following year, the government appointed him to explore Tierra del Fuego.

He traveled aboard the *Villarino* together with captain José Marzano, chaplain José Fagnano, a navy doctor Polidoro Segers and twenty-five soldiers. They anchored in Bahía San Sebastián and immediately began exploring.

One day, at noon, he returned with a few wounded soldiers, three Indian women, also wounded, and six Indian children as prisoners.

He explained that they were attacked by some *Onas* and they defended themselves with guns. The casualties were twenty-six Indians.

Commander Spurr, captain of the *Villarino*, and chaplain Fagnano were furious about the massacre, considering it could have been avoided if he´d just tried to reach a peaceful understanding with the natives.

They continued with their surveys, and some days later they again encountered the Indians. But this time the chaplain and Segers took the initiative and managed to establish an amicable contact with them.

During a third encounter near Cabo Peñas, the soldiers killed two natives and took women and children prisoner.

The last stage of the expedition concluded in Ushuaia.

In 1887 Ramón Lista was appointed to replace Moyano in the governorship of Santa Cruz. When traveling aboard the *Magallanes* to assume his new post, the ship collided with a rock in Puerto Deseado, and capsized. Three of the crew died, and all the cargo on board was lost.

In Deseado there was only a very small colony, founded by Antonio Juan Santiago Oneto, that barely managed to survive. Not only did they have nothing to offer the shipwrecked newcomers, they were really expecting all the provisions that capsized with the ship. Lista sent a party to Punta Arenas to seek help while he went on horseback to Santa Cruz and then on to Lago Argentino to pursue new surveys.

Meanwhile, a group of settlers, afraid that help would come when it was already too late, managed to get a whaler rigged up. Together with members of the *Magallanes* crew, they sailed towards Patagones. They got word to Buenos Aires by telegraph, letting them know about the accident, and returned to Deseado with the help previously requested.

Lista was of the opinion that the settlement in Deseado must be dismantled and the colonists transferred to Coyle and Santa Cruz.

He often wondered if Deseado would ever be apt for agricultural exploitation. He didn´t really think so; on the other hand, he realized that future colonists could make good use of those lands for sheep-raising.

He also described Deseado as a "perennial stream", or "a small current lost in a wide valley".

In spite of his opinion, the settlers decided to stay on, and after twelve years of putting up with all sorts of hardships they were finally acknowledged by the government. The foundation of the town of Puerto Deseado was decreed in December of 1899.

Ramón Lista firmly believed that the natives of Tierra del Fuego were cannibals. Maybe that explains his behavior with the tribes of that region. Besides, his belief was supported by others who had visited those territories.

In *"La Patagonia Central"* he states that the "troglodyte of Patagonia was also cannibalistic".

> *"Therefore –he wrote- I am not surprised that the tekenikas and the onas, descendants of that race, who inhabit a territory even more desolate than Patagonia, still persist with that outrageous and nauseating practice".*

In the report he sent to the Government regarding the "central part of patagonian territory" he stated: "To be slain or subject to indescribable torments would be our likely fate if we should happen to fall into Indian hands; but we were ready to fight".

His views weren´t so radical when it concerned the *Tehuelches* or other peaceful tribes he encountered during his reconnaissance work. In fact, on many opportunities they acted as his guides, and he established a friendly relationship with them. But his general opinion of the aborigines was usually quite different to that of Moyano or the perito Moreno.

Patagonia fascinated him:

> *"Everything here stirs our deepest emotions: sometimes it is the sad barrenness of the plains; or the magnificent chaos of its mountains; and very often, it´s the splendor of the evening calm that we find deeply moving".*

Behind his contradictory nature lay a strong feeling of justice which appears in some of his writings:

> *"The only really important drive in a man´s life is the search of personal wealth, his heart is devoid of hope and strong beliefs; what is not arithmetic doesn´t interest him (...) The outlaw-merchant of Punta Arenas, the greedy merchant of Gallegos, these are the two elements of extinction: what is left by one is taken by the other; they escape from the fire and fall into the embers; the indigenous man belongs to them".*

And he requested that both Chile and Argentina sanction:

> *"a law of agrarian reservations based on the text of the newest law issued in North America in favor of the Sioux"*..

Carlos María Moyano

PATAGONIA

Carlos María Moyano had a profound knowledge of Patagonia and its basic needs. He believed in colonization as the necessary impulse towards progress and development.

A Navy second lieutenant, he was very young —twenty-two- when he joined groups of explorers to carry out specific studies in southern territories. He worked on the *Rosales* under Luis Piedra Buena's command and also on the schooner *Santa Cruz*, with the perito Moreno, where they had to go up-river towing the boat. The horses had been provided by the Indians, after the customary negotiations.

That "business" transaction was carried out with Indian chief Cochigan's wife, María, acting as go-between. During the negotiation she declared that the owner of the horses was the dog beside her and that it would be impossible to reach an agreement without its consent. Obviously, that was the right moment to start handing out the gifts. The presents offered seemed to sharpen María's wit, so when she considered that the dog was agreeable to the deal, they swapped.

That mission took them four interminable months.

"The rope has burnt our hands to the raw —recounts Moreno-, and the thorns have lacerated our feet and legs…" But that didn't mark the end of their sufferings: the relentless cold, the pangs of hunger or physical pain were everyday companions driving them to the edge.

When they almost despaired of reaching their goal they eventually arrived at the lake discovered by Feilberg and found the message in the bottle. They named the lake Lago Argentino, then explored the river described by Feilberg naming it Leona, and finally reached Lake Viedma.

When Moreno was resting on one of the shores of the river Leona he was attacked by a *puma*; it overthrew him digging its claws in his back. Moreno was unarmed; he managed to get up, wrapped a poncho around his arm and started waving a compass; the animal pounced on him again clawing at his arms and legs; finally his friends came to the rescue and killed the beast. The men were tempted to cook the *puma* and use it for a meal, but the stench of the animal finally decided them against it.

They did, though, use its name to christen the river. They named it Leona.

Once Moreno got over his fear and his wounds healed they went on their way.

They discovered Lake San Martín and held their breath when they beheld the imposing mountain peak which the Indians called Chaltén. They named it Fitz Roy. On their return they carried out a survey of the place where the waters originated and the confluence of the Chalía.

Moyano returned to these sites a year later, in the company of Ramón Lista. Together they explored the rivers Santa Cruz, Chico and Chalía, and discovered Lake Quiroga.

One of the most important exploring ventures (which, like many others, was financed by him) was to go over the same itinerary that Musters had covered between Santa Cruz and Chubut. They wanted to verify if it was possible to herd cattle the Indian way, that is by land, instead of transporting it by sea.

This would demand pastures and sufficient water stations. If it were possible (and Moyano was positive about this) they would foster settlements in San Julián, Santa Cruz, Deseado and the bay of San Gregorio.

Some colonists, scouts and a couple of Indians accompanied Moyano on this journey, taking with them fifty-five horses and fifteen hounds. This plan had been previously presented to the Governor of Patagonia, Coronel Alvaro Barros, but as Moyano received no answer he decided to proceed on his own.

At that moment Coronel Barros was worried about England's intentions in Malvinas:

> "England has established very close commercial relationships with the barbarians of Patagonia, whom they treat with fairness and justice. They have therefore earned their trust and always send a few young Englishmen to mingle with the Indians, to learn their language and their habits; and they take to Malvinas an equal number of young Indians who are taught the English language, several trades, music…"

Actually, the same could have been done with our language had Moyano's project been approved, because he had always encouraged friendly relationships with the aborigines. Both he and Moreno had reached an understanding with the Indians who were quite willing to cooperate.

Some even accused the Welsh of providing the natives with weapons.

Continuing with his long itinerary Moyano discovered the largest lake in Patagonia which he named Buenos Aires; then he reached the lakes Colhue

Huapi and Musters, which he surveyed accordingly, and arrived in Rawson three months later.

When the expedition came to an end he drew a map showing the "colonizing route" which would later be used for herding cattle.

But first he organized a sort of "dress rehearsal" and led six hundred head of cattle from Chubut to Santa Cruz. The animals arrived in good shape in spite of the three full months' journey and the fact that at that precise moment there was a war on against the Indians. If Moyano had had a casual encounter with the Indians he would have been forced into an armed battle because, although he was on friendly terms with the *Tehuelches*, the temptation to steal cattle would have been too hard to resist.

Moyano's initiative had very positive results; he proved it was possible to herd cattle by land instead of using sea transportation, thus avoiding the loss of many animals.

In 1881 he went to Europe appointed by the Argentine government to represent the country at the Geography Show, in Venice.

On his return he went back to exploring Patagonia, always with the purpose of discovering places apt for the creation of new colonies.

He was Governor of the Territory of Santa Cruz from 1884 until 1887.

Estanislao Zeballos, who was then Minister of Foreign Affairs, appointed him for a secret mission: he was to lead the Comisión Exploradora de la Patagonia with the purpose of appraising the borderline from the south of the Nahuel Huapi to Paralell 52. Going with him were a lieutenant and twenty-five men; they took horses, cattle, dogs and mules.

His ensuing report proved most useful to draw up the document that Argentina presented at the arbitration courts in London.

Francisco Pascasio Moreno (the "perito")

Francisco P. Moreno was an explorer whose knowledge of geography and anthropology led him to pursue studies in Patagonia which proved to be of great value.

His ideal was to turn Patagonia into an emporium of the south which would concentrate all the resources necessary to promote the development and defense of its territories.

He carried out his explorations some time before the armed victory over the Indians and was very well informed about the "indian problem" whose defeat, as he had predicted, was not a guarantee of civilization.

After his first trip to Nahuel Huapi, he commented:

> "The Indian philosophy as regards the relationship between the "owners of the fields" and the white usurpers justifies revenge; nevertheless, their revenge is not nearly as terrible as ours. The Indian is traditionalist by nature and keeps a vivid memory of the mass murders of his forefathers carried out by Rosas the tyrant; he also remembers the shootings during the "Campaña del Desierto" which took place almost every day over the last twenty years".

Moreno felt his scientific activity was a personal commitment in a country in which the lack of fulfillment he found inconceivable.

He did his job with the idea of progress always lurking at the back of his mind.

The more he explored these southern territories the more he was convinced of the potential riches they contained.

He was a valuable adviser on many different subjects. The "indian problem", the boundaries issue, how to promote industrial and economic growth were, among others, problems to which he dedicated much thought before drawing his own conclusions.

Moreno believed in the possibility of expanding the colonies throughout that vast territory and establishing production centers; of course this would only be possible "if there is a definite change in the distribution of public land which should, in future, be given only to those who are willing to exploit it with their own personal effort".

He strongly supported the establishment of communication routes between the Andes and the Atlantic Ocean and extending the railways from the andean region –including Chubut, Neuquén and Río Negro- to the port of San Antonio; he considered the latter would have the same local importance as the city of Rosario in the north.

Moreno´s scientific contribution allowed for an up-to-date cartography of Patagonia, plus valuable information regarding its natural resources, growth potential and the extension of railways. He could visualize a great future, and his enthusiasm inspired Ezequiel Ramos Mejía, Public Works Minister, to take important decisions, such as hiring the services of Bailey Willis, a North American geologist, to make a feasibility study. The outcome of his work was the famous plan "Ciudad Industrial de Nahuel Huapi".

Moreno also played an outstanding role in the demarcation of limits with Chile. This was a particularly tricky issue, and Moreno played his part with diplomatic cunning and great perseverance. He was an expert on the subject and put across his ideas with great personal conviction. All this must have motivated the English arbiter, Colonel Sir Thomas Holdich, when he wrote to Moreno, in 1902:

> "*I am convinced, and have said so repeatedly: everything that the Argentine Government can obtain west of the division of continental waters is all thanks to you*".

His travels

Moreno carried out two important expeditions to Patagonia (1875 and 1879) and other shorter trips such as in 1873, to Patagones, and in 1874 to Santa Cruz in the company of Carlos María Moyano and a naturalist, Carlos Berg.

He often wondered why there was confusion regarding the names of the different tribes when, in actual fact, they all belonged to the same race, the *Araucano (Puelches, Mamuelches, Ranqueles, Pehuenches, Huiliches, etc.)* His research revealed that the different names were given according to the place they lived in. Therefore a *Puelche* coming from the east may be a *Huiliche* (people of the south) when approaching the south. A *Puelche* considers that all those who live in either of the andean ranges are *Moluches*. On the other hand, the *Moluches* camping in the Chilean part consider *Puelches* those who live on the Argentine side of the Andes.

In 1875 he embarked on a long journey under the auspices of the Sociedad Científica Argentina. His first destination was Las Flores, by train, then via stage-coach to Bahía Blanca, continuing on horseback to Patagones, coasting the river Río Negro up to the confluence with the rivers Limay and Neuquén, and finally reaching the Indian camp of chief Saiyhueque who invited him to be his guest.

Then he went to Nahuel Huapi but the natives forbade his crossing over to Chile. They were afraid he would discover the secret paths used for passing the cattle stolen in the province of Buenos Aires across the Cordillera to the neighboring country.

During his return trip to Buenos Aires he found out that the Indians in Chichinal were organizing a giant *malón*. On the way he met a group of natives and pretended to be a Chilean interested in buying cattle.

- Well...–he asked-...were many christians killed?
- Many, and there was a commanding officer killed too.
- Do you know his name?
- Yes. Turao.

Moreno suppressed a sigh of regret, and thought to himself "Poor Major Jurado...to think he was afraid for my life when he bade me goodbye in Azul...and that I replied: Who knows which of us they will kill first?"

He was also told the coachman had been killed, and how they had slain a "beautiful young girl" who was caught hiding under the stage coach in a vain attempt to avoid being taken captive.

Francisco P. Moreno was aware that those terrible crimes would soon be repeated. He desperately needed to warn people about the oncoming raid. Galloping at full speed and overcoming dangerous encounters with armed Indians on the way, he finally got in touch with the Minister of War in person, and advised him about the *malón*....only they didn´t believe him. They said they were just "scary ideas coming from a frightened young man".

In March of 1876 the "big invasion" took place. Not only was it a gruesome massacre, it also ended in a colossal cattle robbery.

The following year –by this time Moreno was twenty-four- he returned to Santa Cruz and, together with Moyano, they went up river to Lago Argentino and discovered lake San Martín.

In 1879 he was appointed by the Comisión Exploradora de los Territorios del Sur (Exploring Committee of the Southern Territories) to make a survey of the areas between the rivers Negro and Deseado that were suitable for establishing new colonies. Once his mission was concluded, and on his return trip, he went through a terrifying episode.

He was taken prisoner by Saiyhueque´s warriors and taken to the camp in

PATAGONIA

Caleufú. Apparently this operation was in retaliation for the military onslaught during the "Campaña del Desierto". Anyway, the fact was that he, together with other prisoners, were sentenced to death. Such was the rage and fury among the tribe that not even chief Saiyhueque was able to control his people.

Moreno tells how "the vicious Indian witch-doctor declared my death was necessary to expiate the death of the Indians, and that he must receive it in the way of the "bulls and witches", that is tearing my heart out on the river bank".

That same night Moreno saw two Indians crawling stealthily towards his tent. They held knives in their hands, and obviously they planned to slaughter them. They managed to shoo them off but even so, he and his companions –the Indian Gavino and Melgarejo- realized that they must escape, otherwise they would be killed.

They made off while the natives slept, Gavino and Melgarejo on horseback and Moreno clinging on to the horse´s tail. A few stones attached to the poncho would help to erase the tracks. They reached Collón-Curá and promptly built a raft with some pieces of wood they found on the way. They could still hear the screaming at a distance; obviously the natives had discovered their flight, but luckily they had no way of guessing what course they had taken.

The raft was very flimsy. The weight of three men was rather too much for its frail structure, which was at the mercy of the strong current that tossed it around mercilessly. Moreno later wrote: "The Indians would surely find us if we couldn´t make it before dawn". The raft advanced crazily, bumping against the stones. The wounds on the men´s legs took months to heal.

Always fighting to keep afloat, the raft took the course of the Limay and then the Neuquén. Eventually they managed to stop at an islet. The men were exhausted, and Moreno felt severe pains in his back and his waist. They hid the raft, washed their clothes and took a rest. They ate some sheep fat for lunch, and at night they re-took into the Limay on the raft. After four days of carrying on in this fashion the men felt at the end of their tether. Hunger was unbearable, their strength was waning, and they were not out of the danger zone yet. The Indians were still close by, they could feel it. Every night they had to repair the damaged raft. Every night they wondered if they would outlive another day...

Their hope was to reach the big Manzana-Geyú tree and gather some fruit. But the current was so strong they barely got a fleeting glimpse of the tree at a distance. That was on the fifth day. Eventually they saw smoke some miles away; suspecting it could be an Indian snare, they decided to approach without letting themselves be seen. Hiding the raft, they walked stealthily towards the place where the smoke was coming from and there they saw Indian trails, still fresh.

They were so tired they could hardly move. With nothing to eat, they could only drink water to quench their endless thirst brought on by a fever that threatened to destroy them.

Two days later they were too weak to use the raft and decided to continue on foot.. Gavino and Melgarejo walked aimlessly, like zombies, just following Moreno until they let themselves drop to the ground: "We cannot continue, boss… we can´t."

"I´ll never forget that terrible night among the thorns! My men couldn´t sleep, their eyes just stared into the darkness…they seemed dead"

Next morning they barely managed to cover a few yards´ distance. Moreno got a glimpse of a dark bulk lying ahead, and wondered… could it be a fort? Just in case, he unfolded the flag he carried under his arm, tied it to a twig and asked Gavino to wave it from the top of a hill while he fired a few shots. After firing fourteen shots he saw a lot of movement next to the strange dark shape he had seen. Suddenly there were people running all over the place and they were approached by a patrol that appeared from the woods.

The soldiers were preparing for an attack and they were most taken aback at the sight of the flag.

- Who goes there?

- Moreno, escaped from the Indian camp.

The soldiers came to greet them. They offered Moreno a cigar.

- I don´t smoke, my friend, but I would be grateful for something to eat…

Moreno was a cultured man of multiple skills. Well known as a scientist and explorer, during his travels he also proved to be a good teacher and a qualified conservationist. His passion was serving his country in all those aspects that could promote growth and progress. He was totally committed to the protection of the land and the different species that inhabited it, and his deepest desire was to help create natural reserves.

As a reward for services rendered in the demarcation of boundaries with Chile, the Nation gave him –by law N° 4192- some fiscal lands in the Nahuel Huapi area.

> *"I have admired places of exceptional beauty; I have also said in different opportunities that it is convenient for the Nation to own a part of them and keep them for the benefit of present generations and those to come; this is what the United States of America and other countries that own superb national parks have done."*

True to his beliefs, Moreno donated three square leagues that were to become a national park. The Government accepted his donation and promised to turn it into a natural reserve. That was the basis of what would later be the Parque Nahuel Huapi.

Shortly after Moreno went to Europe to carry out specific studies and research. In Paris he attended the University courses given by his friend and teacher, the eminent Pablo Broca. He was also invited to the Sorbonne and other scientific forums. Wherever he went he gained everybody´s liking and respect.

Then he went to London with the idea of gathering the information he needed to organize the Museum of La Plata; his visits to the British and South Kensington Museums helped him investigate the evolution of the human species from an anthropological standpoint.

When he was appointed Director of the La Plata Museum he applied all the know-how he acquired on his trips abroad, and turned it into "the first scientific institution of the country".

And, last but not least, he had also earned the acknowledgement and respect of the Indians.

When Theodore Roosevelt -former president of the U.S.A.- came to Argentina, in 1913, he wanted to meet Francisco P. Moreno to ask him to join him in a trip to Chile and a visit to the Nahuel Huapi. Moreno declined the idea of traveling to Chile -for diplomatic reasons- but proposed joining the North American statesman in Paso Rosales. There he met old friends and word got around that "Tapayo" had arrived. That was the affectionate nick-name -"tapayo" means "dark"- the Indians had given Moreno.

Soon there was a large crowd of natives gathered around the lake, all cheering "Tapayo!...Tapayo!... Tapayo!...". Moreno was dumbfounded. Roosevelt, carried away by the natives' enthusiasm joined them in their greeting with the traditional cry of the North-American red-skins.

Some time after, when Theodore Roosevelt was visiting Paraguay, he wrote Moreno a letter saying:

> "*My dear doctor: not only do I feel for you the deepest respect and admiration, but also personal affection and esteem.*" And he added: "*you have carried out a work that only very few men in each generation are able to perform*".

South America

Venezuela

Guyana

French Guiana (France)

Suriname

Atlantic Ocean

Colombia

Ecuador

0°

Peru

Brazil

Bolivia

South Pacific Ocean

Paraguay

20°

Chile

Uruguay

Argentina

South Atlantic Ocean

40°

80°

60°

40°

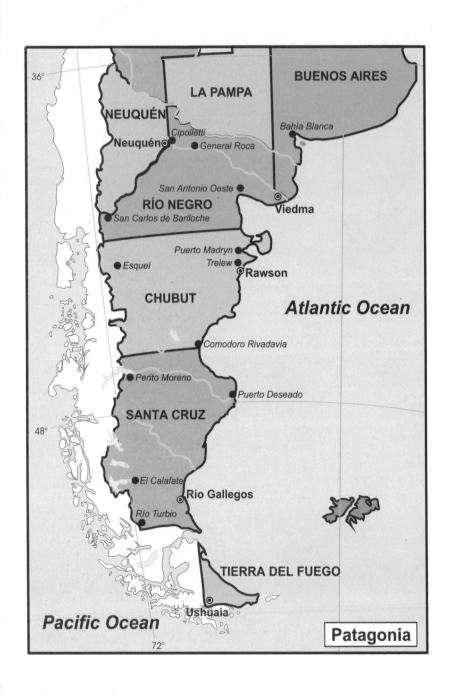

36°

BUENOS AIRES

LA PAMPA

NEUQUÉN

Cipolletti

Neuquén

● *General Roca*

Bahía Blanca

San Antonio Oeste

RÍO NEGRO

Viedma

● *San Carlos de Bariloche*

Puerto Madryn

Trelew

● *Esquel*

Rawson

CHUBUT

Atlantic Ocean

● *Comodoro Rivadavia*

● *Perito Moreno*

● *Puerto Deseado*

SANTA CRUZ

48°

● *El Calafate*

Río Gallegos

Río Turbio

TIERRA DEL FUEGO

Ushuaia

Pacific Ocean

72°

Patagonia

Perito F. Moreno

Orllie Antoine

Hernando de Magallanes

Francis Drake

Cap. Piedra Buena

Patagonia is like a huge scenario with an unending display of unusual episodes and a rich variety of characters: bold navigators, fierce pirates, unscrupulous adventures, devoted settlers, immigrants like the Welsh or the Boers, anxious to live in a place that would show tolerance and respect for their beliefs and traditions… This enigmatic territory made of desert and rock, glaciers rivers of turbulent waters, and the ever present wind, all this suggests a land of violent beauty.

Lewis Jones

George Musters

Juluis Popper

In 1764 Louis Antoine Bougainville, French navigator and writer, together with a group of colonists, settled in the islands he named Malouines.

Top: the second settlement was Carmen de Patagones, founded in 1779 next to river Río Negro.

Left: hamlet and primitive store in the island of Pavón in 1859. These were the only locations with a scant but permanent population within the vast Patagonian territory.

Illustrations of the lighthouse of the ends of the earth in Julio Verne's book published in 1905. This picture fascinated readers from all over the world.

The lighthouse really existed. It was built on the Isla de los Estados in 1884 to guide the ships in stormy waters. The picture shows the original lighthouse, with the staff that had been appointed to work on the island.

In a gesture of good will France donated (1998) a symbolic reconstruction of the lighthouse to Argentina, to be placed in the original location.

The famous Orkeke between two Tehuelche chieftains.

Chief Casimiro, who "sold" the Estrecho de Magallanes to an Irishman.

Painting of Piedra Buena and the victims of a shipwreck he rescued.

Maintenance of the Beagle in the river Santa Cruz.

Top: Charles Darwin admitted that Patagonia held a powerful fascination over him.
Bottom: Robert Fitz Roy, captain of the Beagle, led a dramatic expedition to find the source of the river Santa Cruz. After a strenuous eighteen-day-long walk they managed to get a glimpse of the snowcapped mountains of the Cordillera but, due to their exhaustion, they decided to return. They never knew how close they came to reaching their objective.

View of the Perito Moreno glacier.

Welsh settlers in Gaiman, 1903.

Right: shoveling snow to clear the railway.
Bottom left: typical building in Junín de los Andes.
The villagers lived in almost complete isolation
and led a life of sacrifice and hardships.

Carts loaded with wooden posts and assorted goods in Esquel, in 1930, circulating in front of the well-known commercial firm "La Anónima".

Oil industry in its beginning, in Comodoro Rivadavia. This became a very prosperous activity.

Caravan of carts transporting bales of wool for shipment.

The cabin where Sundance and Ethel used to lived at present. Its ruinous condition is quite obvious.

Sundance Kid and Ethel in New York before leaving for Argentina.

A neighbor described Mr.Ryan (Butch) as a "very educated man. He always put a few drops of cologne in the basin before washing his hands. He always had a book at hand".

Only remaining picture (1903) of Butch Cassidy, Sundance Kid and Ethel during their stay in Patagonia. They lived like ranchers for more than four years in Cholila. Here, Butch with a group of friends who went to visit him at his ranch.

Right: picture of the wild bunch, several copies of which were sent to Argentina by the Pinkerton Agency to identify the outlaws

Bottom: outside view of the Tarapacá Bank in Río Gallegos.

Troops marching on the snow during
the military campaign 1880- that
subjected the Indian tribes and put
an end to their dominion in
Patagonian territory.

Fort in San Martín de los Andes.

Soldiers inside a
telegraph office of the
First division fort, next to
the confluence of the
rivers Río Negro and
Limay.

Popper's soldiers in deadly pursuit of the Indians, one of which is lying dead between the legs of a "hunter".

Right: view of a gold miner's camp.

Bottom left: Popper, facing the camera, with his staff. Bottom right: a miner watching gold-bearing sands being washed.

Top: Martin Sheffiled, west-man who came to Patagonia as a gold prospector and traveled all over its territory guiding expeditions. He had been a sheriff in Texas.
Left: wind-blown tree called "árbol bandera".

Left: scientific explorers on an expedition in 1879, in Choele-Choel.
Right: 1924, one of the last Tehuelche women, in Chubut.

Travelers stop to consider the condition of this very primitive bridge over the river Neuquén, 1925.

Strange picture showing an engine covered by snow, and trying to move on while the peones (who don't appear in the picture) try to clear the railway with shovels.

Sheep-breeding establishment in the extreme south of Patagonia, isolated in the desolate steppes.

1911, two English cattlemen having a conversation beside a "chata" of the Mount Aymond ranch, after delivering bales of wool in the port of Río Gallegos.

Boer immigrants who came from South Africa to Patagonia in 1899.

Part of the Welsh immigration that arrived in 1865 and settled in the province of Chubut, on the Atlantic coastline and also at the foot of the Andean mountain range. During the first church ceremony, the sermon alluded symbolically to "Israel in the desert".

Typical Patagonian city on the Atlantic coast at the beginnings of colonization in Rawson and Trelew.

The "Train of the end of the world", which was used in the past to transport prisoners, is nowadays a tourist attraction in Ushuaia.

Sheep on the route nº 40.
(Gentileza Fundación Germán Sopeña)

Typical farm of the vally of river Chubut. The first Welsh colonists chose this place settle.

12.- WARFARE AGAINST THE INDIANS

War against the Indians, from colonial times until their final surrender: more than three hundred years with episodes of extreme cruelty - A war of extinction in uninhabited territories. Violent appropriation of unclaimed cattle - The "Campaña del Desierto"- The forts

Under Spanish rule it was impossible to conquer the native population of Patagonian territories. During three full centuries there were alternating periods of battles and of relative peace.

Somehow, there was a permanent quarrelsome predisposition –usually the responsibility of the white population- which led to new outbursts of violence. And all that led to fierce reprisals on both sides.

The Spanish *conquistadores* considered the natives had no spiritual life, in fact, they weren´t even human. From that point of view, the only possible fate for the indigenous infidels was complete submission.

But the Patagonian natives were anything but tame. They were a proud race and refused to be held in bondage in the lands they considered their own. They knew what happened to those who let themselves be caught: they were subject to physical torture and forced to hard labor. They had seen plenty of that, and therefore fought fiercely to defend their freedom.

A Spanish government official of the XVIII Century, had said that "the patagonian Indians thought only of hunting and stealing", that "they are unable to keep anything" and that, as they practically lived on horseback and had no way of replacing the horses that died because of their negligence, they had got into the habit of stealing them from the Spanish *estancias.*

Among the aboriginal tribes, the *Araucanos* were the fiercest warriors. According to Alcide D´Orbigny, they had "arrogant manners and were bold, daring, not knowing even the fear of death". And, he added, "All these free men consider themselves superior to the Christians, whom they despise".

The missionary Allen F. Gardiner was shocked at the remark made by an *Araucano*: "My boy is now big, he´s old enough to fight against his father and beat his mother up". Gardiner was convinced that he could convert these natives; he thought their lack of concern for matters such as eternal life or the soul was only due to ignorance. In any case, he soon changed his opinion when he observed that "the *Araucanos* had a marked preference for *chicha* (corn liquor), fighting and raids". He then decided to dedicate his efforts to the mild, amiable *Tehuelches* who lived near the Strait.

The *Tehuelches* were fewer in number and, even though they occasionally took part in some strife against the Christians, they were far from the rancorous belligerence of the *Araucanos*.

Fighting over cattle

Most of the fighting was over the capture of wild animals. The cows, horses and unclaimed sheep that roamed throughout the *pampas* originated from the cattle brought by the Spaniards. According to Félix de Azara, by 1780 they amounted to forty two million head of cattle. Hunting was a popular occupation both among the Indians and the Spanish *accioneros* who had a license to capture *cimarrón* (unclaimed) cattle destined to feed the local inhabitants, or to export hides, tallow and dried meat. The Indians just sold the stolen cattle in Chile.

Between the Indians, the Spanish *accioneros* and the large number of wild dogs that invaded the plains and attacked the animals, *cimarrón* cattle were on the verge of extinction. That induced Félix de Azara to suggest putting poison in the dead animals and thus put an end to the packs of hounds.

When the Indians were no longer able to capture wild animals they started raiding the Spanish *estancias*. In retaliation, the *estancieros* frequently invaded Indian territory violating all the existing treaties. Plunder, looting and manslaughter were the outcome of these Spanish raids which, in turn, originated violent response. And so on and so forth...

Forts were built and special military forces were trained to stop the Indian raids. The authorities even begged the Jesuits to try to convert the infidels, but the priests didn´t dare approach the *Araucanos* whom they considered irredeemable.

Throughout all the XVIII Century battles alternated with periods of peace.

It was with certain misgivings that the Indians observed the foundation of Carmen de Patagones with its fort, in an area that up to that moment they had considered their own. It was a dangerous precedent which, if repeated, could result in the loss of all their territories.

Indian raids, Spanish massacres

In 1780 several Indian chiefs got together and joined forces against their common enemy, the Spaniards. These had shown the most outrageous cruelty towards the natives, taking some of them prisoner and even murdering prominent members of their tribes together with their wives and children. One thousand five hundred Indian warriors, led by the chiefs Callfilqui, Cacique Negro and Guchulep, attacked the town of Luján between the 27th and the 31st of August. It was a blood-bath, causing around one hundred casualties among the Spanish population. The Indians finally retired taking with them prisoners and cattle, although they were disappointed because they hadn´t been able to capture Manuel Pinazo, an important landowner whom they hated. He owned a very large estate -mostly uncultivated land-, and, together with another landowner, Clemente López Osornio, they practiced their own private sport, which consisted in invading Indian territory. In one of these onslaughts they raided the Indian camps of Laguna Blanca Grande and Sierras del Cairú, killing more than three hundred "infidels".

Pinazo took an active part in the defense of the frontier of the province of Buenos Aires. He was also the leader of a group of local landowners who fought against the Indians with the fanatic belief that the "savages" had to be eliminated.

He was famous for his cruelty —once he ordered the killing of all natives over eight years old- and also for his bravery. The Indians never managed to take active revenge on him personally, although they did kill López Osornio on his own land, next to the river Salado. They murdered him with the same cruelty he used when he invaded their camp with a "legal" permit to slaughter every adult native that could be considered "suspicious".

1783 was a year in which belligerence reached one of its highest marks. Indian onslaughts were carried out with unbelievable ferocity.

There had to be an end to this situation, and, in fact, negotiations to reach a sort of peace treaty began a year later, during Viceroy Loreto´s government. An agreement between the Indians and the Spaniards was finally signed in 1790. This allowed for a period of relative peace which favored an active commerce between the natives and the white population.

The Government of May and the Indian problem

When the Government of May rose to power, Mariano Moreno appointed Coronel Pedro Andrés García to study the situation on the border with Indian territory with the idea of working out a conciliatory agreement.

Coronel García went on a caravan to Salinas Grandes. The report he wrote when his mission was completed revealed an original outlook on the problem at stake.

He considered the treatment given to the Indians had been cruel and humanly damaging.

Not only was it wrong to conquer them at the point of a bayonet, it was also useless to expect them to form part of the white society without having been prepared for such a step. They just loss their freedom and had nothing to gain by it.

He believed it was possible to reach a peaceful arrangement on the basis of pacts and agreements that must be kept –with no exceptions-, and an acknowledgement of the Indian rights. This implied accepting the fact that the natives "worship their cattle and their properties".

A year later, by initiative of Coronel García, a group of Indian chiefs were invited to pay their respects to the revolutionary government. Feliciano A. Chiclana greeted them with these words:

> "Without delving into the causes that have separated us up to now, let us just say that we are all branches of the same tree...Friends, countrymen, brothers, let us unite to form one sole family."

Peace lasted for quite a few years; the ranchers extended their lands beyond the Salado river, and some Indians even worked as *peones* (rural workers) in their establishments.

But not all Indian chiefs thought alike. For instance, Yanquetruz led an assault against the town of Salto, destroying everything and killing many people. Martín Rodríguez went after him but failed in his capture, so he could think of nothing better than to take revenge on some peaceful tribes which were on good terms with the whites. That of course provoked the fury of all the natives, who got together and organized one of the biggest and most devastating raids.

Again Coronel Andrés García was asked to negotiate a peace treaty, only this time he was not successful.

Martín Rodríguez led another battle against the natives, which was absolutely in keeping with his own particular ideas:

> "*Experience shows us that there is only one way of dealing with these men; we are convinced that this war must pursue one ultimate goal: their total extinction.*"

When Rosas was in power, he tried to "buy" peace paying the Indian chiefs wages. That brought about favorable results from the economic and military point of view and many leagues of the desert were conquered. But operations were not properly concluded on the border with Chile and new payments had to be made to pacify the *caciques*.

The great warriors

Calfucurá was one of the most famous *Araucano* chiefs. He was already powerful in Rosas's time but it was only after the "tyrant" was overthrown that he became overtly ruthless with the *huincas* (white men) and led a devastating attack on Bahía Blanca. According to Mitre, Calfucurá was the leader of the largest confederacy of tribes in the Desert ever known after the conquest.

Francisco P. Moreno referred to a terrible battle that took place in 1855 in San Antonio, an *estancia* south of the province of Buenos Aires. Taking part were Chacayal and Saiyhueque, both young warriors at the time. Only one soldier got out of there alive. Saiyhueque had commented that the Indians wet their hands in white blood and ate *caritun de huinca* (an expression that means to eat raw meat, which is used to describe the great massacres of christians).

Moreno presumed it was some sort of

> "*vague reminiscence of olden days when they used to practice cannibalism. I know of cases where, in the frenzy of manslaughter and bloodshed, some Indians drank blood and ate the heart of the white enemy.*"

There was a generalized pessimism regarding the fight against the Indians.

Estanislao Zeballos wrote:

> *"The indians sauntered along the land like invincible conquerors,*
> *the army was demoralized, the spirit of the National Guard was*
> *terrified and the neighborhood in a state of grief and desolation".*

In the 1860´s the *Araucano* raids and onslaughts had become even more violent. They invaded the villages burning down the houses, destroying whatever they found on their way, killing people... the terrified villagers fled from all this riot, afraid they could end up captives of the savages.

It was not till 1872, in the battle of San Carlos (west of the province of Buenos Aires) that Calfucurá was defeated for the first time, by the combined forces of the army –under the command of general Ignacio Rivas- and of the Indian chief Catriel.

Although Calfucurá never really recovered from the shock of his defeat and died one year later, his men kept the war-loving spirit alive. Lieutenant Eduardo Ramayón wrote:

> *"The Indians, with horses that seem made of steel racing across the*
> *enormous expanse of the infinite pampas (...) will always have the*
> *country in a state of panic."*

It was only during the government of president Avellaneda, when Adolfo Alsina was Minister of War, that a definite plan of action to conquer the *Araucanos* was drawn up.

Even so, in December of 1875 the Indians carried out the "big invasion" which resulted in one of the biggest cattle robberies in history: one thousand head of cattle.

Alsina, the strategist

Coronel J.S. Daza wrote about Alsina:

> *"The first task undertaken by Alsina was to lift the army´s morale*
> *(...), to provide the cavalry corps with the necessary modern*
> *equipment: lance, saber, revolver and armor; to furnish the different*
> *units with transport facilities; then he introduced new war tactics,*
> *supplanting the old-fashioned defense system with a new concept,*
> *which was to take war to the Indian camp itself".*

Alsina first extended the frontier and in 1876 he took over Carhué and then Puán, Guaminí and Trenque Lauquen. The following year he won a battle against the forces commanded by the Indian chiefs Pincén, Catriel and Namuncurá. But he was suddenly taken ill and transferred to Buenos Aires, where he died, on the 29thof December 1877.

He was a man with original ideas. He invented an ingenious defense system, which was a ditch that would block the Indian incursions. The excavation of this five-hundred-kilometer-long ditch took two years, and it extended from Italó –south of Córdoba- to Bahía Blanca. The project also included forts every five kilometers.

Enter Roca

Adolfo Alsina was supplanted by general Julio A. Roca, whose ideas were quite different to those of his predecessor as far as strategy was concerned. He decided to lead an active campaign against the Indians in 1879 with a totally offensive plan. He also introduced a new weapon, the Remington, which would turn the tables in his favor.

The Remington was largely responsible for the Indian downfall.

President Avellaneda put on pressure:

"This handful of savages must be forced to surrender without delay"

A powerful army of several thousand well-armed men were to fight against a scarce two thousand natives bearing spears.

General Roca had a very clear objective: the extermination of the Indian forces.

The way to achieve his goal was through massive and simultaneous onslaughts from different positions. Four months afterwards he counted four hundred dead or wounded Indians, and approximately four thousand prisoners.

He then launched another attack with five military units, and in 1879 they advanced taking Azul, then Río Negro and Neuquén.

The opposing political parties described Roca´s expedition as an "army parade", and Sarmiento wrote:

"It is shameful to think that a powerful military force of almost eight thousand men has been used to fight against a scant two thousand Indian lances".

The end of the war was declared in 1884: Namuncurá had surrendered in March, and one of the bravest chiefs, Valentín Saiyhueque, sent one of his sons to inform General Vintter that he was willing to give himself up. That actually occurred on the 1st of January 1885, in Junín de los Andes.

Some pathetic episodes took place during this war, one of them being the capture of Indian chief Orkeke, who was already a very old man. He had earned the liking and respect of men such as Musters, Lista, Moyano and Francisco P. Moreno. When he was taken prisoner to Buenos Aires Ramón Lista paid him a visit and offered him to return to Patagonia. The old chief rejected the offer, and he died shortly after, a stranger in an alien city...

Coronel Lino Oris de Roa had captured Orkeke´s tribe and then sent their chief to Buenos Aires. Coronel Vintter had stressed that "no harm must be done to the Indians".

Nicanor Larrain, a traveler who actually saw the *tehuelches* boarding the ship, wrote:

"A crowd of Indians came on horseback, praying and singing a strange, monotonous music in an unknown language. All Orkeke´s tribe was there: seventeen men and thirty seven women and children".

He was surprised by

"the resigned acceptance of their fate, the kind look shown by the men, a certain haughtiness in the women, and above all the mournful singing of the crowd that repeated: "le queneque yaque de ya; le yu, le yu, quelelo..." A most sad chorus that led to thinking what right had we to cut these people off from their everyday life?"

No more significant battles occurred during these events; the Indian bravado had disappeared together with the proud warriors brandishing their spears. One last attempt was carried out by the *Araucanos* of the *Foyel* and *Incayal* tribes who, with the support of a group of *Tehuelches*, fought against the troops led by Lieutenant Palacios in the plains of Appeleg.

The Indians were once more defeated...

Coronel Rufino Ortega wrote, in his Memoirs of 1883, a description of Indians in combat:

> *"Light on his feet and bold, quick and violent when charging against the enemy, able skirmisher when in battle; he can retreat and then reappear by surprise when everybody least expects it. He can walk for days and never seems to be tired; he can spend days without rest nor food; he can put up with anything when on horseback. His thick skin makes him insensible to the roughness of the weather; he was born to fight and shall live making war; maybe he will end up like just another ignored hero.*
>
> *They get together in small parties riding on first-class horses, move around with astounding swiftness and can easily fool us in our pursuit; they know how to survive anywhere: the plains of La Pampa, the snow-capped mountains of the Andes...it's all the same to them who have learnt how to live off the fruits of whatever soil they tread on. Always short of provisions, because they prefer to travel lightly. They have learnt through experience one of the main principles of a guerrilla war, which is to damage the enemy without engaging in a definite battle, carrying out missions where skill and cunning can prove more useful than a powerful display of arms in open combat. They learnt the hard way, suffering persecution and constant harassment.*
>
> *All this explains why these groups, led by clever, cunning "caudillos" have been so active and inflicted so much damage on the organized army in a war that lasted –unbelievably- far too long".*

Soldiers and their women

New territories were discovered during the desert war. But, of course, the fact of their being unexplored posed countless difficulties both to riders and their horses.

The soldiers lacked almost everything. Very rough living conditions were maybe softened by the company of the women who went along with them. These women were generally considered "of doubtful reputation" and consequently looked down upon. They were submitted to the Army Code and treated like soldiers. They ate the same meager rations, led the horses, suffered hunger, thirst, extreme cold or heat. Sometimes they went on for days with nothing but a few weak "mates" to calm the pangs of hunger.

Sarmiento thought very highly of these women. He was full of praise for their:

> "...intelligence, suffering and faithfulness. They were a powerful support, helping in the maintenance, upkeep and discipline of the forces. The soldiers didn't even consider deserting, everything they loved was there, in the camp".

They had to cook, wash, care for the sick and the wounded, and even fight if necessary. It was their duty to:

> "respond to an officer or guard's first summons; be present at all the dances or parties; attend the wakes and burials where they would pray for the soul of the deceased. No matter what the circumstances were, they were always there".

Alfredo Ebelot, an engineer who always expressed his admiration for their courage and resistance, wrote:

> "They have been company and also help to the Argentine soldier in that border war where most would have succumbed had it not been for their presence."

And when they were not present, the soldiers missed them terribly; they either deserted or simply dragged themselves around, unwashed, untidy and looking miserable.

These women were, then, the faithful and caring companions of these poor frontier soldiers.

The latter were described by Commander Manuel Pando as follows:

> "If an outsider had happened to watch us in formation, he would probably have wondered what horde of criminals we belonged to. No two soldiers were dressed alike. This one used his rug in the way of a "chiripá"; that one lacked the jacket; some wore old, twisted boots, others just a pair of "alpargatas"; and those over there had their feet wrapped in pieces of hide; these here were barefoot..."

Obviously, serving in the army wasn't very tempting in those days. Something had to be done to draft soldiers, and so the Law against Vagrancy was invented. This law enabled the judges to accuse anybody they wanted of vagrancy, and so this person was forced to join the frontier army groups. Where did they look for their "prey"? Usually in the *pulperías*, which were regularly raided by the police.

Commander Manuel Prado felt sorry for the simple soldiers, and stressed the fact that:

> *"they had conquered twenty thousand leagues of territory but that enormous fortune went to the hands of the land speculators who bought them without any effort nor personal work (...) Seeing how these public lands were shamelessly "granted" in extensions of thirty or more leagues to some privileged few, and watching their obscene, greedy look, it's no wonder then that many would feel like cursing this glorious conquest..."*

Of course, there were cases where quite the opposite took place.

Juan Napal, -an Indian who fought against the army under the orders of the brave Indian chief Nahuelquir and later became an ally of general Roca- claimed the title deed of a plot of land of a quarter league. And many other natives in Cushamen followed suit. Nahuelquir, who had been on friendly terms with the Perito Moreno and Clemente Onelli, thought there would be no difficulty in obtaining their land. But when he wanted to approach them, it was too late.

> *"It's been twenty five years since I started claiming these title deeds* -he complains-. *That's all I'm asking for, for myself and my family. But, since don Clemente Onelli died, I have no more friends left in Buenos Aires. I'm getting old and wouldn't like my family to be deprived of this little farm which has been my home for more than forty years and that I dearly love."*

He'd worked that land for almost half a century and begged to be acknowledged as its rightful owner. But nobody heard his plea...

13.- PIONEERS

The frustrations of Ernesto Rouquaud and his family – Fortunes and misfortunes of Gregorio Albarracín and his young wife – The extravagant Julius Popper and the gold rush - Tierra del Fuego is invaded by greedy gold-diggers

It´s hard to imagine that anybody would dare to pack up and leave the comfortable life of Buenos Aires to go and settle down in Patagonia; not in those days anyway. Let´s just remember that in that endless territory the only existing towns were Carmen de Patagones, then much further south, -on Pavón island- the village founded by Luis Piedra Buena, and the Welsh colony.

Two of the most touching attempts at colonization took place in the province of Santa Cruz.

The frustration of Rouquaud

Ernesto Rouquaud was a French businessman who was going through a difficult financial moment (in 1872) due to the commercial dead-end brought on by the yellow fever in Buenos Aires. He had been quite prosperous thanks to the production of grease and oil in the factory he owned in Avellaneda. His products had been awarded prizes in the Exposition Universal de Paris, in 1867, and he had important projects in mind for the future. Until the outbreak of the epidemic and its devastating consequences.

A conversation held with Luis Piedra Buena (who had settled down in Pavón island three years back) made him think that installing his industry in Santa Cruz could be a good idea. We can guess that Piedra Buena may have described a very favorable situation because he himself lived and worked in his beloved Patagonia. And we can also imagine that Rouquaud was confident that, given an opportunity, his attributes as an entrepreneur would yield profitable results in this new and tempting enterprise.

The fact was that he launched out into a larger project than the one in Buenos Aires.

First he wrote to the government requesting he be granted some land to establish a fishing industry and a factory for the production of oils and by-products. Part of that land would be destined to the settlement of new colonists.

His request took a long time in getting through Congress, in fact, he even had to contend with a French competitor, with whom he eventually became associated.

When Rouquaud finally decided to settle down South, he proceeded to sell off his factory, mortgage and sell real estate properties and other holdings, and then organized the transportation of machinery, equipment and personnel to Santa Cruz.

Part of Rouquaud´s family (Ernesto, his twenty-one year old son, and two of his daughters; twelve-year-old Luisa, and twenty-six-year-old Eloísa, whose husband had died recently) and several workers with their families traveled on board the *Roebuck*, reaching Cañadón Misioneros in February of 1872.

Ernesto Rouquaud arrived six months later, together with his wife, Luisa Perichón, and six more children.

He soon found out that river fishing was no big deal and that sea capture would necessarily demand special ships. On the other hand, his situation became more complicated because Chile was against the settling of colonies south of Santa Cruz –a territory the Chileans considered their own- until the formal demarcation of limits was established.

All these setbacks affected the people´s morale. Some of them found the environment depressing, many even returned to Buenos Aires.

Rouquaud was most alarmed by this turn of events and traveled to Buenos Aires to request protection against the Chilean threat. Sarmiento offered the Government´s support in these circumstances.

Upon his return, Rouquaud was greeted with the terrible news that Pablo, his seventeen-year-old son, had drowned while trying to rescue a boat.

Things were never going to be the same for Ernesto Rouquaud, who never really recovered from this loss.

Then came the period of waiting. Like so often in the past, this group of people, stranded in the midst of this desolation, had all their hopes fixed on a ship that was to bring the help the Government had promised.

And so they waited for the *Brown*. Unfortunately, the ship was so old and run down that it couldn´t make it to Santa Cruz and returned to Patagones. And so again they waited.

Some time after, the schooner *Chubut* finally made it, commanded by Guillermo Lawrence, with Feilberg and Palacios as Second Lieutenants.

After unloading the equipment and other items they raised the Port Captaincy and then hoisted the Argentine flag.

Thus, national jurisdiction was formally established in Santa Cruz.

Shortly after the departure of the *Chubut* on its return trip, the colony in Santa Cruz was visited by a Chilean gunboat, the *Covadonga*. The officers seemed bearers of good will and were soon on friendly terms with the Rouquauds, who organized social gatherings and dinner parties to entertain them. The officers were delighted with their new friends and enjoyed the company of the young ladies of the family, who were both cultured and charming. In spite of the hosts´s misgivings about the presence of Chilean sailors in an area that was still in dispute, they had nothing to say against their guests. Indeed, they did their best to make their stay a show of Argentine hospitality.

They had a farewell party the night before leaving, at the end of which they sang the Chilean and Argentine national anthems.

The Chilean ship was about to weigh anchor when desperate screams were suddenly heard, begging for the ship's doctor´s presence. They quickly disembarked and discovered Mrs. Rouquaud had suffered a heart attack.

In spite of the specialized care afforded by the ship´s doctor, the lady died four days after.

The *Covadonga*, disobeying orders, had delayed its departure these days so that the doctor could assist Mrs. Rouquaud. After her death, the hundred crew members were arrayed in a row with torches, lighting the path through which the coffin was carried, towards the chapel where their son, Pablo, was buried.

Initially, the Rouquaud establishment —which was still not producing- rounded up approximately one hundred people. But after so many setbacks, the people became discouraged and gradually left Santa Cruz. Some of them returned to Buenos Aires, others went to Punta Arenas.

When the *Chubut* returned, only the Rouquaud family and some household help still remained.

The French businessman went to Chile to request authorization to set his establishment in motion. The Chilean government denied permission, at least until there was a formal decision concerning the limits affair. Instead, the authorities offered Rouquaud an indemnity of ninety thousand "patacones", which was the estimated value of the installations. Félix Frías, the Argentine ambassador, advised Rouquaud not to accept that offer because it was an unsuitable antecedent for the country. The Frenchman complained bitterly; he felt he was caught in the middle of a diplomatic battle that would lead him to inevitable bankruptcy. In an attempt to cool things down, the ambassador promised to negotiate an adequate compensation with the Argentine government.

Rouquaud went back to Santa Cruz to dismantle his establishment and then returned with his family to Buenos Aires. Only the eldest son, Ernesto, stayed behind, with the purpose of going to Patagones to sell the machinery and equipment and then go back to Buenos Aires with all the cash he could collect.

Ernesto sailed on board the boat *Pasquale Quartino* with captain Lawrence, who was not only a friend of the family but also a qualified seaman. What Ernesto didn´t know was that Lawrence had been dismissed from his former post because of certain mental problems.

Whatever happened on that trip will always remain a mystery. But the fact is that the ship that left in 1874 bound for Patagones never showed up. Nobody ever found out what had become of Rouquaud´s eldest son, or of Captain Lawrence…

The moment Ernesto Rouquaud got to Buenos Aires he tried – unsuccessfully- to obtain the indemnity that Félix Frías had promised him in exchange for the one that the Chileans had offered and that he, following the ambassador´s advice, had rejected.

For years he was sent from one office to the other, but nobody paid any heed. Nobody cared…

He died a poor man.

After his death his daughter, Julia Rouquaud de Maillé, wrote:

> *"My father has died a poor man…why? Because Argentina hasn´t acknowledged its debt. We honored our commitments…why does this country not do the same? We could say the Chileans drove us*

*out, but then, they were our political enemies. Our country has
done much worse, it has ruined a man, destroyed his family, his
well-being and his whole future. That has been our reward after
having undergone all kinds of difficult situations".*

On another opportunity, Julia showed her resentment towards official
indifference:

*"I know people who never even attempted to colonize, who never
did anything good for the people –we even know some who did a
lot of harm- and yet the government has awarded them rights over
what they didn´t own and what wasn´t their due".*

Francisco P. Moreno had his say about Rouquaud and his predicament:

"Rash haste can cause much damage to those who pretend to carry out
ambitious projects in these territories without knowing what they´re up
against...

(Rouquaud), seduced by promising reports, launched his project without
the necessary thought and premeditation. He didn´t calculate the risks. His
establishment was on an altogether too big a scale for these regions..."

Gregorio Albarracín

Official propaganda during the 80´s urged people to emigrate to the
furthermost parts of the country. One of the suggested places was the
territory of Santa Cruz. In order to promote colonization in that region a law
was passed by which each family would receive one league of land alongside
the river Santa Cruz, five hundred sheep, three mares, two cows, a wood cabin
and working tools. After five uninterrupted years of working this land the
colonist would be entitled to be its legal owner. The cattle and the tools were
a loan, therefore they had to be returned to the state after that five-year
period.

Luis Piedra Buena, who had always been an active promoter of the
colonization of that region, persuaded lieutenant Gregorio Albarracín to settle
in Santa Cruz. Albarracín had fought in the war against Paraguay and later in
the Desert War against the Indians, during which he requested being
discharged from the army to pursue agricultural activities. He then consulted

Piedra Buena about his plans, who firmly advised him to carry out his project in Santa Cruz.

He then proceeded to register in the Lands Bureau where he was informed that approximately ten families were due to travel to that budding colony. He embarked with his young wife on board the *Santa Rosa*, in 1880. He soon found out that, except for don Ignacio Félix Peralta Martínez and his son Jacinto –sheriff and secretary of the new colony- and the Captain Francisco Villarino, they were the only colonists on board.

Upon reaching their destination Gregorio Albarrracín observed that, apart from the group of people who lived on Pavón island, there were only a few members of the sub-commissions of Misioneros and Deseado.

His wife, María Salomé González de Albarracín, who was eighteen years old at the time, remembered:

> *"How sad were those lands! When we disembarked, we were most impressed by a legend carved on a piece of wood: "Adiós tierra ingrata de guanacos y pingüinos" (Farewell, mean lands of penguins and guanacos). Afterwards we found out it had been written by a Navy officer who had been stationed there some time back".*

When Albarracín received the five hundred sheep assigned to him, only half were still alive. Nevertheless, he was obliged to sign the receipt for the value of five hundred, otherwise he would have to return to Buenos Aires on that same ship. The ex-officer agreed to do as ordered, and prayed he would be able to overcome this setback.

They installed in a *rancho*, having the family of Gregorio Ibáñez as neighbors. Gregoria Ibáñez, mother of five, was a Chilean and the only white woman in the neighborhood, so, obviously, she made friends with young Mrs. Albarracín.

On a cold winter morning, when the couple was already properly installed, Gregorio Albarracín found a flock of around seventy sheep near his yard. They were from Malvinas and had obviously not been sheared for at least two years. He guessed they must have strayed from Punta Arenas. He thought it was a good opportunity to cross them with his "merinos" from Río Negro and obtain a new breed that would be better adjusted to that region.

Supplies came from Buenos Aires by boat. Once the boat took more than

PATAGONIA

nine months in arriving, so Albarracín had to travel to Cabo Vírgenes –about five hundred kilometers away- to buy provisions at a gold-digger's camp.

Everybody looked forward to the arrival of the ships, not only on account of the supplies but also because it was a break in the monotony of everyday life. Parties and all sorts of social and cultural events took place in the Albarracín homestead. Piedra Buena attended one of these getherings and he actually became god-father of Francisco Luis, first son of the Albarracín couple.

Francisco Luis's birth came as quite a surprise, because he arrived much sooner than was expected. At the time, Gregorio Albarracín had traveled to Misioneros, Juan, the young *peón* was out herding cattle, and doña Gregoria, who had promised to act as midwife, wasn't there either. So, María Salomé was completely alone when she started feeling the symptoms of imminent birth.

Precisely at that moment, when we can imagine poor María Salomé's despair, somebody knocked at the door.

It was Poivre, a little old Frenchman who had come from Punta Arenas and just happened to pass by.

María Salomé recalled:

> *"He came to my house to see if he could stay, precisely at the moment when my son was being born. I begged Poivre to go to the river bank and call Ibáñez asking him to please cross his wife over by boat. She arrived hours after the birth, and by then my husband had returned."*

The Albarracín family lived in a two-room shack made of wood and corrugated iron sheets. It was placed right in the middle of three hills. "The churning wind enveloped our house with clouds of dust and sand making our life impossible". In those days, whenever the couple went out walking they held hands, because "that was the only possible way to walk".

The couple had a *peón*, a young lad called Juan Arriyaga who had come with them from Buenos Aires. One day, Juan disappeared. That made Mrs. Albarracín very uneasy, specially because her husband had been away for two months -he had gone to Chubut with the idea of buying cattle from the Welsh-, and Juan was the only company she had.

She ran desperately to the river side and there she met John Williams, the sub-prefect, and some sailors, carrying the lad's dead body, that they had discovered at low tide.

Meanwhile, her husband hadn´t reached Chubut because he´d been taken ill and was forced to return. He never really recovered, and due to his health problems they finally decided to return to Buenos Aires, after four years of living in these implacable surroundings.

Of course, they gave the State back what was due.

"All that was left over, my husband sold to Gregorio Ibáñez, who paid us over the years, little by little, with fruit, feathers and quillangos, which he always sent to me in Buenos Aires, even after my husband had died, until he cancelled his debt.

The truth is –remembers María Salomé- whatever profit we made was from buying feathers and quillangos from the indians and re-selling them to old Poivre.

We left Cañadón Pescadores in May of 1883".

The gold rush

In 1876, near Cabo Vírgenes, a small fishing cutter commanded by Gregorio Ibáñez –a seal fisherman who worked for Piedra Buena- was shipwrecked. When the crew went looking for drinking water and started digging,...lo and behold! They found gold! The glee they all felt was nothing compared to the excitement caused by the shipwreck of another ship –the *Arctique*- some years later in those same shores.

The ship was carrying valuable cargo and over two hundred men were sent from Punta Arenas to rescue the goods. In those days, rescuing was usually followed by looting; this time there was a double prize, because apart from the booty found on the ship there were plenty of gold nuggets lying around on the beach.

From that moment on the place became a major attraction for gold prospectors from all over the world. Groups of Dalmatians arrived from Buenos Aires, then sealers from North-America and Chile, and all of them joined the group of gold-diggers that had set up camp in Zanja a Pique, Lucacho and Cañadón de los Franceses. From then on everyone worked by himself and at his own risk, always on the look-out. There were neither demarcations nor concessions. No authorities either. The gold-diggers invented a washing system with gutters on a slant with holes at regular periods; this allowed the water to flow and wash the nuggets that would then deposit at the bottom of the basins.

A Rumanian engineer

Every Patagonian event was represented by some original or heroic character who left his particular hallmark as a symbol. In this case, our hero was undoubtedly Julius Popper, a Rumanian engineer specializing in mines. Word had got around that there was gold to be found in Patagonia, so after finishing his studies in France he quickly moved out here. First he stayed in Buenos Aires where he got in touch with powerful people who could be of use to him in the organization of his project. Popper created the company "Lavaderos de Oro del Sur", -some of whose members were Ayerza, Lamarca, Le Breton, Ruiz de los Llanos, Ramos Mejía and Cullen- and traveled to Cabo Vírgenes. There he developed a particular aversion towards the crowds of gold-diggers, who were, in his opinion, ruthless and ill-natured people.

Julius Popper was a clever public relations man who knew exactly who to contact and what must be done in order to achieve his goal; there was always some ulterior motive lurking behind each project of his, which was in this case the building of his own empire.

Following the tradition of many southern pioneers, he left most of his scruples and careful considerations to one side and launched right into action.

He was allowed to have a group of fifteen men working under his orders; these men wore uniforms and bore arms "just in case there was an Indian onslaught". He was also entitled to explore Tierra del Fuego "from a scientific point of view". During these explorations he discovered the river Grande, and, on his return via San Sebastián, he installed his gold-washing establishment, which yielded two pounds of gold a day, in a site he called El Páramo.

Those who saw the gold dwindling down in Cabo Vírgenes tried to approach El Páramo but were warded off by Popper´s guards. They resorted to shooting as a way of discouraging intruders. Some of the gold-diggers complained to the Chilean authorities and asked for protection, but the government officials shrugged them off, it was Argentine territory and there was nothing they could do about it.

The local authorities disliked the eccentric engineer, who proceeded with the utmost impunity and total independence, always protected by his private army. He was well known as an egomaniac of haughty manners and had already made quite a few enemies among the local public officials who resented his enterprise and determination. They were also afraid of him, being aware that he was capable of driving out or even murdering Indians or intruders without batting an eyelid.

Popper didn´t accept competition and imposed his own code of justice, which basically consisted in justifying all that suited his interests. He went to the extreme of minting his own money and printing his name on stamps.

Governor Félix M. Paz refused to meet Popper´s request of a police station in El Páramo, because -he explained- he lacked personnel. He also refused to admit Popper´s legitimate rights on concessions that had been granted to him in Buenos Aires, such as the one in Bahía Slogget.

There is evidence, though, that governor Paz´s behavior gave him no right to question Popper´s ways. The governor had been mixed up in the side-tracking of certain funds assigned to the province´s budget. And he was also accused of selling coal from a ship that belonged to the state.

The company Lavaderos de Oro del Sur was dissolved in 1890, and Popper remained sole owner of the installations. Besides, he convinced the national Government to grant him a concession of eighty thousand hectares, with the purpose of "educating the natives, who would be granted some lands once they had been properly civilized and converted to the Christian faith". But when he asked for an extra three hundred and seventy-five thousand hectares the Government said no. Governor Cornero, who shared with his predecessor the same dislike for Popper, must surely have had a say in the matter.

Why did the "dictator" Popper have so much influence in Buenos Aires and Punta Arenas?

He obviously had the knack of getting exactly what he wanted –for example, lands given in concession- without any of the usual tiresome red tape and under his own terms.

Remarkable!

But, why? Many of those who wondered were simply short-sighted in their analysis. They didn´t take into account the magnetism of his powerful personality. Above all, because the "porteño" élite had a soft spot for all those who were imbued in european culture and showed charm and talent. And Julius Popper definitely qualified to be the "enfant gâté" of Buenos Aires's social circles. He had graduated in Paris, mastered several languages –Spanish among them-, had "savoir faire" and engaging manners.

Lucio V. López spoke highly of him, as "a forerunner of the victories of civilization against barbarism and of society against the desert". And he added:

> *"He spoke all languages, wrote ours with elegant grace, with a most colorful style (...) Some pages written by Popper remind us of Edgar Poe and Mark Twain at their best. He was witty and sarcastic, he had, we could say, an original sense of humor".*

Another explanation for Popper's popularity was the fact that he was a successful man.

As opposed to many other gold prospectors who were still hopelessly operating in places which were already exhausted, when he visited Tierra del Fuego for the first time he knew exactly where to look for the precious metal.

Popper was the only one who developed a rational and systematic exploitation of the areas that were richest in gold reserves. He was also the only one who made money out of this activity. He proved to be a resourceful man when he invented the sand-washing machine which "extracted" 99,6% of the gold from the sand using much less water and in record time. Other advantages of this machine: it eliminated the mercury baths and it was easy to carry; usage demanded no previous knowledge. And, most important, it made embezzlement impossible.

Popper also invented other washing gadgets which could be used on the beach.

He traveled regularly to Jujuy and Bolivia where he operated other mines. Intruders tried to make the most of his absence breaking into his camps, and some of his *peones* did the opposite, deserting to go and look for gold on their own. Others escaped stealing some of his gold.

So, on his return, he had to make discipline prevail and punished the transgressors:

> *Sailors who had deserted from their ships, escaped prisoners, people of different races who could either live in total confinement or out in the open air who had come from Punta Arenas to "take a*

look".

Julius Popper was afraid his *peones* would find life in the "open air" more gratifying –and profitable-. And he had to do something drastic to prevent the intruders from stealing his oxen. So he would start a shooting demonstration.

He would line his soldiers up, wearing some Hungarian army uniforms which he probably thought more imposing, and he would start ranting and raving, getting worked-up in some wild speech.

> *"You have been the first to break into the mystery surrounding these regions! You have conquered these virgin lands from the savages and have proved to be worthy representatives of civilized men! (...) all these events that make your parents proud of you and honor your children, will always be present in our memories (...) Look at that flag, showing the white of justice that guides your weapons, and the blue of the skies protecting you all the way...!"*

His rough-hewn mercenaries were not as excited as their boss; they were actually rather worried about what could happen to them in the immediate future.

They could do nothing but listen and wait for the order to attack the bandits. The strategy was to take the clandestine camps by surprise and start shouting and shooting at the baffled occupants, who were mostly:

> *"Criminals and brigands of different nationalities. All armed with Winchesters, of course. Some dressed in rags, others barefoot, not a single one of them resembled another. They yelled, laughed, gesticulated, and suddenly the scene changes. This bunch of crooks moves like one sole body, like a nest swarming with snakes. Terrible screams can be heard: "on guard!..."*

Precisely when Popper's soldiers fired their guns.

Some lay dead on the ground, others although wounded, ran towards the Chilean border.

And there were still others who, according to Popper,

> *"knelt down on the ground, their arms spread out, eyes popping out of their sockets, trembling and begging forgiveness: ¡Ave María!. One man screamed out in despair:*
> *"I´m not like the others...I´m a carpenter...I´m poor...I worked the gold with Governor Paz..."*

According to the amount of *bandidos*, Popper calculated how many of his private soldiers were made to appear:

> *"Had the criminals taken a good look at those soldiers, they would probably have been surprised to see that [the weapons] were wooden sticks, that underneath the uniforms there were vegetables instead of meat, and that what looked like a head was just a bundle of rags... they were just scarecrows, the manikins of El Páramo, the establishment's last resources!"*.

The action was not limited to the criminals and gold-diggers. As has been registered in photographs, Popper and his army also engaged in some skirmishes with the Indians.

All these anecdotes show up the more theatrical aspect of Popper's complex personality, which had to do with his imperial fantasies and dictatorial ways.

Nevertheless, whenever he had to use his intellect he proved to have a clear insight about the southern territories, and his own personal ideas.

In his interpretation, Tierra del Fuego was divided in two ethnographic areas:

> *"On one hand, the archipelago, inhabited by alacalufes and yaganes, misbegotten indians who seem doomed to disappear due to their weak constitution, who live in canoes and fish as a way of survival.*
>
> *On the other hand we have the island of Tierra del Fuego, which the natives call Ona-sin (country of men). It is inhabited by onas, vigorous looking Indians with a strong constitution who resemble the tehuelches because of their height. Their angular faces and sharp features remind us of the North American Indians.*
>
> *Far from the descriptions afforded by some cabinet wise-men, this race fully represents the primitive man in its maximum expression of moral and physical evolution"*.

Popper said that at first he was unable to establish a friendly relationship with the Indians.

> *"At first I thought they were intellectually under-developed. Since then I have proved that they are not only capable of achieving high levels of perfection but they also have noble feelings, sound*

common sense and a kindly disposition. They can even forgive their
enemies to the point of protecting the race that harasses them,
leading shipwrecked people stranded on the beach to places where
they can get help.

They are affectionate parents, showing tender love for their
children, as the children show tender love for their parents; they
carry mourning for their dead painting their face black [...] They
wash their bodies and faces very often and dry with a soft yellowish
moss that hangs in long rows on the branches of the fueguian
beech-tree.

"They are thieves!" complain the ranchers who live in the Chilean
part of the island.

"They steal our sheep and destroy our fences!" That's all very true,
but let's just for one moment put ourselves in the Indian's place.
For many centuries the Ona has hunted the few wild guanacos of
the island without horses (because there are none); without
trained dogs, because the local breed, which resembles the canis
dingo of Australia, is only good to be used as a pillow, or as a
heater. The Ona, bearing his bow and arrows, and hiding behind
the bushes, waits sometimes several days for his prey, which is
common property, it belongs to the whole tribe. And, alas! if the
arrow were to break, because it takes one whole day to make
another one. In the meantime, the women and children eat tucu-
tuco; the island is swarming with these rodents, the native's last
chance for survival.

And then suddenly, something happens that will disturb their life as
nomad hunters. A strange enigma appears into their lives. Men of
an unknown race approach their shores, disembark and, in one
sole operation, place three, four, five thousand sheep, and white,
fat, tame guanacos on their lands.

It's a new and totally unexpected scene: on one side, two thousand
hungry Indians without food; on the other, five thousand sheep and
only three or four men.

The Indians wonder: "What does this strange phenomenon mean?"
They fail to find an explanation for this strange apparition; they
consult the old wise men, and the witches...No, they say, these

things do not belong to our traditions. Are they messengers of some mysterious entity, some superior beings that have come –at last!- to make up for all the things that the indians have always had to suffer? But, how is it that only three or four strange men can eat five thousand white guanacos all by themselves? That´s impossible!, exclaim the indians, and immediately launch themselves on the sheep and catch some; surely such a lucky event deserves a banquet!

But a terrible blast interrupts the party, terrifying shrieks filling the atmosphere. Here and there, mortally wounded men drop to the ground. A brother, a son...Mercy! For pity´s sake!, scream the terrified Indians. We didn´t mean to offend you! All in vain, because those men don´t even listen to them, and if they did they still could not understand them. So the Indians, scared out of their wits, grab their bows and answer the unexpected attack with a shower of arrows. But the enemy is already out of their reach; the Indians have run out of arrows and try to advance so as to trap the enemy into a hand-to-hand combat, but it´s impossible. The far-reaching bullets kill from a distance...

So the Indians flee. Weak, exhausted and out of weapons, they hide. They need some time to think things over, they still can´t quite make out what´s happened to them, why they have had to suffer this terrible injustice in their own hunting lands; they surmise that the forced appearance of the white guanaco in their domains is a sign of a cruel, endless battle that is yet to come, one of the many in what they suspect will be a war of extermination.

Whose side does injustice take? The Indian´s side?

Isn´t the government supposed to instill notions of cattle ownership in the Indians before allowing the introduction of sheep in their lands?

Is it not a duty of the government authorities to provide the Indians with means to make a living instead of barging into their lands and taking away from them the guanaco, which is the only animal that provides them food and clothing?"

Popper delivered this dissertation in Buenos Aires and finished it with the following story:

*"We were chasing a guanaco when suddenly we came face-to-face
with a crowd of around eighty Indians with their faces painted red;
they were completely naked, and distributed in small groups
behind some bushes. The moment we set eyes on them a shower of
arrows fell on us, around the horses. Luckily no damage was done.
The next moment we had dismounted and were answering the
Indian aggression with our Winchesters. It was a weird combat.
While we fired our guns the Indians lay flat on the ground and
stopped shooting arrows; but the moment we ceased fire the
whistling sound of arrows piercing the air would recommence.
Little by little we managed to place ourselves with the wind in our
favor, and the Indians were gradually forced to retire (obviously,
no great damage can be caused by an arrow flung against the
wind). The bodies of two dead Indians remained on the ground".*

A close-up picture of those two dead Indians magnified the image Popper
had fostered of himself as a ruthless pursuer of aborigines and transgressors.
He wasn't particularly worried about this, in fact, he considered himself above
good and evil, and highly valued his rational intellect in this region swarming
with coarse, greedy people.

He was always on the alert, nothing escaped his shrewd powers of
observation. He analyzed nature, and studied men's reactions and behavior.
Many of his actions, -which could be considered shocking by ordinary
standards- were in keeping with his eccentric and arbitrary personality, so he
always felt justified in doing whatever he did.

He could be described as an illustrated tyrant.

His conference at the Instituto Geográfico Argentino –July of 1891- was
remarkable. He unfolded his acute observations about the *onas* as well as a
brilliant assemblage of geographic, geologic, meteorological and agricultural
knowledge. He gave the name of Mar Argentino to the waters between Cape
Horn and Tierra del Fuego. And he captivated the audience with his lively
descriptions which showed the depth of his geographical knowledge:

*"It is very difficult to give a complete picture of Tierra del Fuego in
one brief sketch, because it is a country full of surprises; it is the
land where the polar animals greet those of the tropics; where the
call of the Antarctic penguin meets the prattle of the Equator
parrot; it is the country of many topographic varieties, which has,*

in proportion, more vegetation than Mexico, more views and landscapes than Norway and Switzerland; in an extension smaller than that of Portugal it concentrates more contrasts of geography and hydrography, of meteorology and ethnography than in all the continent of Australia".

Popper was born in Bucharest in 1857. He lived in Argentina since 1886 until he died, in 1893.

He was living in Buenos Aires at the time of his death, and left quite a few debts.

Gold was just another Patagonian fantasy that was blown away by the never-ending wind.

Most of the characters in this drama ended their days buried somewhere in these regions which never satisfied their great expectations.

14.- OUTLAWS AND THIEVES IN THE PATAGONIAN WEST - · THE GOOD AND THE EVIL

The worst kind of crooks operating at the foot of the Andean mountain range - The arrival of North American outlaws, ranchers and cattlemen - Butch Cassidy and the Sundance Kid. Contributions made by the Newberys and other countrymen - The border police after Wilson and Evans - The English outlaw Helen Greenhill Beckar - Sheriff Sheffield and the legendary plesiosaurus

At the turn of the century, the vast regions ranging between the territories of Chubut and Santa Cruz were chosen by outlaws and thieves as a safe place where they could settle down and operate without running the risk of being discovered.

The inhabitants were few and lived in total isolation. And, as far as the police were concerned, they didn´t show much interest in keeping an eye on their new neighbors or tracking them down.

The cattle-thieves were mostly Chilean, they roamed around stealing cattle to sell in their own country. These brutal, uncouth men hid in the ravines waiting for the right moment to pounce on their prey while the scared settlers kept an armed watch over their cattle and belongings.

Asencio Brunel was an Uruguayan who became very well-known as a horse-thief. He´d been in different places, always running away for one reason or another. From Malvinas he went to Punta Arenas; there he got mixed-up in a murder so he escaped to Patagonia, where he stayed for several years and stole horses for a living. Even though he was sent to prison on many opportunities, he always managed to escape. Everyone suspected there was some sort of police corruption behind this because he always showed great generosity towards his captors.

One day he was identified by Karl Führ, a German who ran a lodge in Lago Argentino and a raft-service that took people across the river Leona. It was precisely during one of those crossings that Führ recognized Brunel. In an instant the German had drawn the Winchester he kept hidden under his clothes, disarmed him, tied him to a horse and delivered him to the nearest police station. Shortly after that Brunel was seen enjoying his choice food - mare´s tongue- in absolute freedom, and taking up his favorite sport -horse-theft- with great enthusiasm.

In Río Gallegos he was accused of murdering Máximo Formel, a landowner whose dead body appeared in a cart that had no horse attached to it. The Buenos Aires newspapers "La Prensa" and "La Nación" demanded the immediate capture of this outlaw.

In Chubut, Indian Chief Kankel´s people were fed up with Brunel, who´d stolen their horses in many opportunities. So one day they cornered him, tied him up hands and feet, loaded him on a mule and rode for twelve whole days to turn him over to Governor Tello.

Due to the prisoner´s expertise in getaways and that he was capable of committing murder or any other crime, he was fettered during the day and put in the stocks at night.

He looked wretched: bristly hair and beard, an intimidating stare, covered in tatters and pieces of filthy hides.

Brunel respectfully begged the priest to hang a crucifix round his neck. The priest felt sorry for him and asked the warden to take the fetters off.

And that was how Brunel fooled Chief Kankel and Governor Tello once again: the thief, who had been so secure in the prison of Gaiman, managed to escape and get lost in the night.

Only this time the people responsible for his escape were punished: the warden, called Martínez, was suspended from his duties for a month; and the sergeant and another officer suspected of complicity were dismissed.

The *Tehuelches* were very disappointed. They would have gladly got rid of Brunel themselves. Turning him over to the authorities meant giving up that personal pleasure. Now that he was again on the loose, they took the decision to track him down once more…only this time they didn´t capture him, he was shot down by one of Kankel´s men.

That was the end of Asencio Brunel, but not of the crimes and robberies. Nobody suspected that Brunel and the likes of him had certain nice-looking, smart North Americans as dangerous competitors.

There were many North Americans in Patagonia. Some were first-class people, like the Newberys and other ranchers and cattlemen who made a position for themselves thanks to the efficiency shown in managing their affairs and plenty of personal hard work.

And there were also the other kind…

Decline and fall of the North American gunfighters

The patagonian West had the reputation of being a gloomy no-man's-land. Quite the opposite of what was happening in the North American West, where the industrial boom was producing extreme changes in those lands which had been a kind of fief commanded by gunfighters and bandits. Progress requires peace and quiet, so the outlaws found themselves besieged by the forces representing law and order. They were harassed by detectives of the Pinkerton Agency, and sought after by hired killers and bounty hunters who worked for the law. For example, E.H. Harriman, the owner of Union Pacific, hired the unscrupulous Joe Lefors to eliminate the Wild Bunch. Lefors caught Tom Horn, got him drunk and wrenched a doubtful confession of guilt from him, after which he sent him straight to the gallows.

In those days, railway guards and Pinkerton style detectives weren't too worried about being methodical sleuths, rather they adopted the ways of efficient, cold-blooded man-hunters, also called bounty hunters. It made no difference to them if they caught their men dead or alive.

The outlaws were aware that they had many things in common with those who were after them: they were expert riders, had excellent horses, were good shots and were equally ruthless. Little by little they were being surrounded by them. And the gang broke up. Some of them were shot, others were hanged, some "joined" the army and a few emigrated.

Bill Carver, a member of the Wild Bunch, was famous for shooting with both hands. He was shot down together with George Curry, during an attempted robbery of a bank in Texas where they'd killed the sheriff.

William Ellsworth Lay (Elza Lay, or Elzy) or William McGinnis, the strategist of the group, was in prison. Thomas "Black Jack" Ketchum had the messiest hanging ever seen in the Wild West: he was sentenced to die in the gallows, but the fall was so long that his head got lopped off.

In the meantime, the head of the gang, Butch Cassidy (his real name was Robert Leroy Parker) was evaluating the situation. He was certain that if the hunters found him they would fill him up with lead, hands up or otherwise. If by chance Butch Cassidy had ever wanted to mend his ways seeking redemption, that was no longer possible, at least in the United States. He had too many crimes to answer for, and besides, he had also brought about the disgrace of many sheriffs who had been committed to tracking him down and had failed. He guessed that instead of capturing him "dead or alive" they would "arrest" him already dead, as a way of getting even for the humiliations he had inflicted on them. So, after evaluating the situation he faced, Butch Cassidy decided to emigrate.

That was the end of the Wild Bunch and the fame gained in countless bank and train robberies. That was the end of a profitable activity which brought them thousands of dollars. Of course, the booty was spent with such speed in whorehouses and gambling that they always had to go back for more.

But no more "coups" were possible.

The time had come to move on.

The educated gunman

Cassidy wasn´t a bully, neither was he an expert fighter. And nobody knew if he was a good shot or not. So nobody could quite understand why he was such a gifted leader.

He was brought up in the belief that there were answers to every question and logical explanations to every mystery. That gave him power, and that was the reason why he was respected among the group of tough, hard men.

He belonged to a family of practicing Mormons. The sermons he heard in church during his childhood and adolescence trained him in the use of rhetorical speech which proved very useful when dealing with his wild henchmen. At least, if they were hard to convince he managed to confuse them. We could say that the basis of his great friendship with Elza Lay was that they formed between them the perfect team: Elza Lay was the brain of the bunch and Cassidy always found the way to reach unanimous approval in all the coups they planned.

William Goldman, who carried out an eight-year-long research of Butch Cassidy´s life before writing the script that originated the famous film, was fascinated by Butch and Sundance. He considered that

"...they both carried out what Gatsby was only able to dream of: to *repeat the past. No matter how famous they were in the United States, they were even more so in South America, where they became a legend: "Yankee Outlaws". Maybe that was what so fascinated me in their story. We all want to recover the past... They made it come true".*

Goldman then told that before leaving for South America

"The three spent a few days in New York. There are some wonderful pictures of their visit [...] One of Butch and his friends' weaknesses was they loved having photographs taken".

One of these –which became famous- was a full-length portrait of Sundance and Ethel posing like a formal, traditional married couple.

As far as Ethel was concerned, she was not so young when she started working in the oldest profession and not too old when she gave it up.

In New York they had a wonderful time. Went to all the shows and theaters, ate in the smartest restaurants. Both men pampered Ethel, and they gave her a present of a gold watch from Tiffany´s.

Joseph G. Rosa, another historian of the Wild West, reported that the trio had spent some time in Preston, Lancashire, Great Britain, visiting some of Cassidy´s relations before traveling to South America. But he gave no further details.

Other writers surmised the group of outlaws could have gone to Australia to join the gold-searching parties, or even to South Africa to try their luck with diamonds. At least in both these countries they could speak English.... At first nobody mentioned Patagonia, maybe because it sounded so strange and hazardous.

Indeed, one wonders what drove them to choose such a remote location.

Could it be that they knew police forces down there were scarce and incompetent? Or maybe they had information regarding the great farming establishments owned by clever *gringos* -mainly English- who knew how to get rich. And besides, there were already plenty of cowboys from Texas and Kansas working in Chaco, Entre Ríos, Buenos Aires Province and a few in Patagonia, who wrote to family and friends back in U.S.A. suggesting there were good opportunities for anybody skilled in rural work.

Butch didn´t improvise this move. On the contrary, he had calculated every detail with utmost care. Part of the money stolen (fifty thousand dollars) from the Great Northern Express, in Montana –holdup carried out in "partnership" with Ben Kilpatrick (The Tall Texan), Harvey Logan (Kid Curry), Jim Thornhill, Harry Longabaugh (Sundance Kid) and O.C Hanks- was destined to finance his transfer to Patagonia.

Some authors also state that the money Cassidy and Sundance brought with them (thirty-two thousand dollars) came from the First National Bank robbery in Winnemucca, Nevada, in September of 1900, that is, before the train robbery. But then, is it possible that their share of the money could have lasted so long?

What actually did survive the passing of time since the coup in Winnemucca was the picture that hangs ostensibly on one of the bank´s walls, where Cassidy, Sundance, Kilpatrick, Logan and Carver pose, looking very smart and solemn.

They were so sure of themselves that they got careless and had this picture taken "just for kicks" in a studio in Fort Worth, Texas. The studio had the picture on display as a sort of promotion. One day, a detective passing by the shop recognized them, so he bought several copies and sent them to the Pinkerton Agency.

On the other hand, the bank also thought promotion would come in well and had the photo enlarged and put in a fancy frame, hanging it where it could attract people´s attention.

Meanwhile, hundreds of copies circulated with the WANTED sign on them.

Even to this day there is no tourist visiting Winnemucca that fails to go to the bank to get a look at the famous picture.

Landing in Argentina

The outlaws´ first stop was Buenos Aires. They stayed at the Europa Hotel, deposited the money in the Bank of London and even had the chance of chatting with the North American Vice Consul, George Newbery. They met him in his dentist´s consulting room, which he shared with his brother Ralph, also a dentist and father of George Newbery, a pioneer of Argentine aviation.

The newcomers were thus able to collect valuable information regarding Southern Patagonia, more precisely the region close to the Andes where the Newberys had their lands, near the Nahuel Huapi.

And they found out many things that would prove of interest in their future business concerns.

The Newberys

The Newberys were the sons of an English homeopath who had settled in New York. That´s where Ralph and George were born. Ralph was the eldest of the two. He ran away from home at the age of fourteen to enroll as drummer in the Yankee army during the war. His parents would have wanted him to study Medicine but he preferred a shorter career and became a dentist. He chose to live in South America, and, after visiting Brazil, decided to finally settle down in Argentina, where he married a girl of French origin.

President Roca, who was a regular patient of his, urged him to buy lands down south. He was convinced that those regions would be very prosperous in the near future. Ralph "bought" the idea and immediately wrote to George, his brother –who was still in the U.S.A.- inviting him to share this promising business.

George disembarked in Buenos Aires in 1877 with his dentist´s degree, but his interests lay in those far off, fascinating patagonian lands.

They engaged cowboys from Texas to work their lands, but these soon sought the way of becoming independent and settling down on their own. In Nahuel Huapi, Ralph Newbery, in partnership with John Crockett, began to export cattle to Chile. They chose Jarred August Jones, a skilled drover, to take the cattle across to the neighboring country.

J.A. Jones, -also called Juan Jones- came to Argentina together with his friend John Crockett and settled down in 1889 next to the Nahuel Huapi on the Neuquén side. He founded the *estancia* Tequel Malal and was one of the first to introduce wire fences. He was well-known for his generous hospitality, and counted, among many other guests, personalities like Ramón Lista and the "perito" Moreno. He actually provided Moreno with several horses to use in the Limits Committee, free of charge. In return, Moreno carried out personal negotiations on his behalf with the Government and convinced the authorities to sell around ten thousand hectares to his Texan friend.

Jarred August Jones married Barbara Drakslor and had a charming, large family.

In 1913 he went to Texas to visit his relations. On the way back he passed through Detroit with the idea of buying a Ford T. The firm made him a tempting offer: if he bought two cars they would give him a third as a gift. That was the reason why he returned to Argentina with three Ford Ts.

The North Americans Jarred A. Jones, Ralph and George Newbery were the first landowners in Nahuel Huapi. Many of these stories are recounted by Diego, George´s eldest son, in an entertaining book called *Pampa Grass*.

George Newbery married Fanny Taylor, the daughter of a North American clergyman, and traveled to the Cordillera de los Andes with the idea of settling down. As was customary in those days, they went first by train, then on a horse-driven wagon and then on horse-back. They got lost, so George decided to climb a mountain to have a general look around and try to find the right path. In the meantime, he left his wife alone with the horses for a couple of days. They finally managed to find their way and were able to continue their journey. But that incident revealed what a fine, courageous woman George had married. She was the first white woman to settle in those regions.

That was only the first, and certainly not the last hazardous adventure. Once, they were returning from Chile across the Paso Puyehue, which was used exclusively by natives. Of course, it was an *Araucano* who guided them. At the end of the way they found themselves in the northeastern part of the Nahuel Huapi, and George saw no other alternative than building a canoe to be able to cross that immense lake. So, using a hatchet and some fire, he "emptied" a tree-trunk and improvised a boat large enough to hold himself, his wife and the Indian. They sailed across to the opposite shore. But then they still had to walk several miles to reach the *estancia*.

Someone asked George what would have happened if they had been caught by a storm in the middle of the lake and had to face high, impetuous waves, but he got no answer.

George Newbery explored lakes and forests. He was the first to sow salmon and trout in several rivers and also encouraged the exploitation of wood.

He proposed a plan to regulate the water flow of the Limay River, and was, in general, an enthusiastic promoter of growth and development throughout that territory.

He was a great friend of "perito" Moreno and they both yearned to create a natural reserve on the style of Yosemite or Yellowstone.

Being always worried about the possibility of an accidental fire burning down the woods, he created the forest warden post, which operated on a private and volunteer basis and consisted in protecting the integrity of the forests. He was named protector *ad honorem* of Forests and Reserves.

His *estancia* –eleven thousand hectares- was first called Traful and then changed its name to La Primavera. That's where he died, in 1933.

His elder brother Ralph, who had become a very rich man, suffered a big drawback when he sent a large drove of cattle across to Chile and it was caught by a terrible storm. All the animals were killed. In order to cover the investment he had to sell his lands and the rodeos and lost practically all his fortune.

There were already rumors of gold in Tierra del Fuego, and Ralph thought that if he got enough of the valuable metal he could quickly get his fortune back.

Unfortunately, the extreme cold and the harsh living conditions, together with the disappointing results of his new venture, proved to be too hard to bear. They put an end to his life.

On the way to Cholila

Butch Cassidy's name in Argentina was James Ryan; and Sundance Kid's was Harry Place.

Cassidy's new alias was "in honor" of James Ryan, the sheriff who imprisoned the young Pennsylvania-born gunman –still called Harry Longabaugh- who would later adopt the name of the prison of Sundance City where he had been locked up. Place was the Kid's surname on his mother's side.

Cassidy and Sundance had plenty of time to talk over their plans during their ride to Cholila. Both knew plenty about farming, they were good breeders (specially horses) and expert horse-breakers; they definitely knew how to round up a good herd of horses. In fact, in many opportunities they had succeeded in escaping from their pursuers thanks to their excellent horses.

Milton Roberts, chief of police of Esquel, told about the time he approached them one day that they were camping near Cholila. They invited

HISTORY, MYTHS AND LEGENDS

him to have some coffee, and he had the chance to admire the beautiful horses they had tied up next to the tent. He sat down for a chat and found out that they were planning to set up a farming establishment: they intended to buy some sheep, cows and horses and hire a couple of farmhands.

He met them again several times, and the conversation was usually about horses: breed, blood, types, characteristics... Roberts was aware that these two men were expert guides. By the way they spoke he gathered they had no difficulty in finding their way out of tricky marshes, cragged mountains or dense thickets. Besides, they were first-class hunters.

In Cholila –a village quite near the frontier with Chile- ice-cold rain and a piercing wind prevail during the harsh winters. On the other hand, spring and summer are usually mild and pleasant. The newly-arrived foreigners were pleased to note that the exuberant pastures were practically uninhabited. The first to settle in that region was Ventura Solís, a Chilean who had been guide in one of "Perito" Moreno´s expeditions in 1897. Then several of his countrymen followed suit and also some Argentines, Sixto Gérez and Agustín González, among others.

One year after the North Americans´ arrival, (1903) the first private school was founded in Cholila. Sixteen pupils attended, and classes were held in Sixto Gérez´s house. The teacher, Daniel Arnoldo Hodge, had specially come over from Neuquén.

Butch Cassidy spent the first winter on his own: Sundance and Etta had traveled to the U.S.A. and would be back in spring. During that period he registered – in the Dirección General de Tierras y Colonias- the ownership of around four thousand hectares of land in Cholila under the names of Santiago Ryan and Harry Place.

Cassidy spent a great part of his time surveying the land, trying to fit into his new role as stock farmer and analyzing the market. Bruce Chatwin reproduced the letter Butch Cassidy sent Mrs. Davis and which is exhibited in the Historical Society of Utah. Concerning his new destination, he wrote:

> *"The only possible industry is, for the moment, cattle-breeding, and there couldn´t be a better place than this to carry it out. I never saw lands with such excellent pastures and with hundreds of kilometers that are still not colonized. [...] It is about one thousand six hundred miles away from Buenos Aires –capital city of Argentina- and more than four hundred from the nearest railway station or*

port. On the other hand, one must only cross the Andean mountain range –one hundred and fifty miles) in order to get to Chile".

When the Chilean government inaugurated a new pass, Cassidy calculated that the following summer they would be able to reach Puerto Montt in four days instead of the two months it took when using the old road.

"This will be very advantageous for us because Chile buys most of the meat we produce and we can carry our cattle across in the tenth part of the time we needed before, and without weight loss".

As we can see, Cassidy was a shrewd businessman when it came to evaluating the market.

He also wrote that he chose Cholila after visiting "the best cities and sites in South America", although we figure this may have been exaggerated.

"This part of the world seemed so great that I settled down –for good, or so I think- and I get fonder of it with each day that passes. I own 300 head of cattle, 1,500 sheep, 28 saddle horses, two farmhands who work for me, a good four-room house, a shed, stable, coop and some hens. The only thing I lack is a cook, I am getting to be a seedy bachelor and sometimes I feel very lonely".

The Sundance-Cassidy-Ethel trio led a peacefully discreet social life in Cholila. Their neighbors held the foreigners in high esteem. They found the three of them educated and gentle-mannered, and had a special liking for Butch who was great fun, and the life and soul of all the parties. Ethel (also called Laura Bullion) with her worldly ways and her attractive looks always shone in the naïve awkwardness of these small-town social events.

They felt a certain admiration for her skills as an amazon and her expert marksmanship. "The lady cut her hair very short and used a wig, –remarked Mrs. Gérez- she dressed like a man".

They always used the same target –a corner post- for their shooting practice. Every time they carried out the same routine which was an awesome spectacle in town: both men shooting with both hands at full gallop and holding the reins with their teeth. Their horses had been carefully trained to put up with the vibrating stampedes.

Ethel spoke Spanish, which made communication much easier. They gradually broadened their social circle, establishing relationships with people of other colonies: Welsh, a few Englishmen, Chileans and native-born of the region. During a trip to Nahuel Huapi, besides visiting George Newbery they got in touch with some Texan cowboys that had been engaged to work in that area, and were also invited by Jarred August Jones to stay at his place for a few weeks.

In return for his hospitality, Cassidy invited the Jones family to stay for some time at his house in Cholila.

But, in the same way that it´s hard to keep a secret, it´s also difficult to remain hidden for very long. In the long run, somebody´s bound to discover the truth.

In their case, they were recognized by some fellow countrymen –Walk, Manning, Kemper, Fingler, Dragler, among others- who were landowners in the outlying Nahuel Huapi. And we could surmise that Newbery and Jones were duly informed as to their true identity.

The same goes for John C. Perry, a Texan former sheriff who unexpectedly turned up at Cholila with his wife, with the idea of settling down. He often visited the trio at their house and did business with them, trading cattle. Nevertheless, his discretion was remarkable: no need to bring up things of the past now that these people had become hard-working cattlemen, and maybe even law-abiding citizens… Perhaps Perry spoke about these things with his fellow countrymen during his frequent business trips to Nahuel Huapi.

What drove all these North Americans to this silent complicity with the outlaws?

Was it the fact of being so far away from home, the homesickness that could lead them to see in these fellow countrymen, not criminals, but friends in need?

Could it be that sharing the native tongue and the spontaneous comradeship that binds men in alien lands created long-lasting ties and new loyalties that couldn´t be broken?

Who knows…

The Places and their intimate friend Ryan (many considered the group a *ménage à trois*) were held in great esteem by the residents of Cholila and neighboring districts.

Even the Governor of Chubut, Julio Lezama, took a liking to them. So much so, that during the summer of 1904 he was their guest and slept in a room of the cabin that they had built following the style of the houses in the Far West.

It was during the Governor´s visit that Sixto Gérez gave a party in his honor. The Governor danced a *samba* with Ethel whilst Sundance played the guitar.

The Governor was absolutely convinced he had been dancing with a charming "belle" of rural society in the U.S.A.

It´s possible that this bucolic environment evoked in Butch Cassidy far-off memories of his youth in Utah, when he was just a mixed-up teenager of a peasant family. His parents owned a very modest farm in Circleville, and that´s where he had learnt to ride and break horses, look after and feed the animals, till the land and sow, dig irrigation channels… but, not much of a future in all that. His parents were austere settlers of Scottish origin who were always struggling to rear their eleven children. Very little money and a lot of hard work, that seemed to be the essence of their life. From their standards, we could guess that survival and prosperity were equivalent terms.

That humdrum everyday life in a world so full of temptations drove him to rebel against the strict precepts of their Mormon upbringing. He soon chose to live as an outlaw. He ran away from his parents´ farm and joined Mike Cassidy, a bold young horse thief who was also very good with his gun. He adopted his "alias" after him, the man who initiated him in crime.

Maybe hidden deep down inside there remained just a trace of that puritan small farmer, although by then his farm was a proper ranch with cattle and the works. He could be a full-fledged cattleman and become prosperous and lead a quiet life surrounded by people who respected him. Could he possibly settle down? The landscape fascinated him…

They lived in Patagonia for almost four years, always devoted to rural work. But, quoting Daniel J. Gibbon who was a close friend of theirs, Sundance Kid never fully adjusted to that lifestyle and —maybe prompted by Ethel Place- was always wanting to leave.

Every now and then they traveled to Chile, Esquel, Colonia 16 de Octubre, Trelew or Nahuel Huapi, where they met with friends and countrymen. It was their way of breaking the monotonous routine of country life.

They bought horses from the "Compañía de Tierras Sud Argentina de Leleque" and Sundance broke in some magnificent specimens.

They had managed to assemble a considerable amount of sheep, cattle and horses, and had obviously improved their status as cattlemen. Now they traded with important *estancias* and agents, some of them from Buenos Aires.

However, they never felt much enthusiasm for private property. It was as if being landowners bored them. Risk was what they really enjoyed. It was only when facing danger or persecutions that they felt fully alive. The excitement of living on the edge seemed to fill that empty void they occasionally felt when they acted the part of respectable citizens.

Besides, Sundance Kid felt real pleasure in squandering money, and Goldman very accurately transmits his annoyance on seeing Bolivia. He said: "And here, where are we going to spend our money?".

Once, when they were returning from Punta Arenas, Chile, they passed through Río Gallegos and camped nearby. They were interested in buying lands in that district, so they chatted with some of the locals trying to gather as much information as possible. They never stopped asking questions about the conditions of the outlying roads, the topography, the crossings and fords. And they made careful scrutiny of all these spots before returning to Cholila. They passed unnoticed through Río Gallegos. They took note of all the places where they could get fresh horses, and the exact placing of the outlying roads and little secret paths that could come in handy and whose existence was ignored by others.

Soon after they registered at the best hotel in Río Gallegos –Hotel Argentino- and the following day they opened a bank account in the Bank of London and Tarapacá. They became members of the Club del Progreso and immediately contacted people who could inform them about land for sale, locations, prices, etc. etc. They behaved like well-off ranchers and were very generous with tips.

Soon, everybody was aware that they had deposited seven thousand pesos in the bank and that they were bringing more money in, enough to cover their investment. They also consulted the bank about receiving money orders from the U.S.A. and about practically anything that could be of interest to prosperous investors.

The rumors and provincial small-talk did the rest.

They got in touch with all the right people and informed them that they were partners of an important stockbreeding company in Río Negro which had plans to expand their operations in that district. They were very careful not to mention Chubut. Only Río Negro and Neuquén.

They also went in for some extravagant behavior that both intrigued and amused the neighborhood: they used to come into town or leave at full gallop, apparently for no reason at all.

Coup in Río Gallegos

On Monday 13ᵗʰ of February 1905 they withdrew from the bank the seven thousand pesos they had in a joint account. They explained the money was to close a deal that evening in the Club del Progreso.

The following day, a cold and windy day, the "two rich North Americans" went to the bank just on 3 p.m. The assistant manager, Mr. Arthur Bishop, and the cashier, Mr. Alexander McKerrow, both English, were the only people present in the hall. They both stood up, eager to please their very important clients. Much to their surprise, they suddenly saw two Colt 45 guns pointing at them and heard a voice ordering "hands up!". By the descriptions it was Sundance who, standing on the counter, pointed his gun at the two frightened men and ordered Mr. Bishop to open the safe.

The assistant manager decided to cooperate because, as he later explained to the police, they had threatened to kill him if he refused. So he began to empty the safe and put the money in a bag Cassidy handed over to him. To that they also added the money that was in the drawer under the counter. They asked the manager for the key to a metal box but he –stuttering and very pale– said he didn´t have it. So the robbers took the box with them.

One of them, presumably Cassidy, went out into the street, mounted his horse and placed the bag beside him. He called out to Sundance "Lets go!". And Sundance, who had been keeping watch on the clerks, calmly left the bank.

Then they left at full gallop but, as that was a daily routine that everybody had grown accustomed to, nobody gave it second thoughts.

In the meantime Ethel had unobtrusively left the hotel early so as to have the first group of fresh horses ready. As had been previously arranged, they had different groups of horses stationed in different places of the itinerary designed for their escape. They made sure that all communication between the chosen sites would be interrupted by shooting at the telegraph wires.

They headed for the ford of the Río Gallegos river and crossed it at Güer Aike, stopping at the Sutherland *estancia* for a change of horses and to pick up some packages with supplies of food and horseshoes which they had left in the cook´s keeping. Nobody knows whether the cook was an accomplice or if he just did them a favor, unaware of the real motive behind his holding their belongings. Besides, how could one possibly refuse a favor to these nice *gringos* who were so generous with tips!

Meanwhile, the town was in an uproar. Much excitement, who could have thought it possible!, indignant men running around, surprise... A posse of police and citizens was organized to chase the *bandidos.* Although everybody suspected the search would be both lengthy and dangerous.

Days went by and not a clue, not even a trace that would encourage them to continue.

The North Americans had excellent horses waiting for them at strategic points, apart from the seven that they stole from the Woodman and Redsman *estancia.*

Help was requested from the Chileans and neighboring villages. Patrols were sent from San Julián, Santa Cruz, Puerto Deseado, and two groups from Río Gallegos.

For more than twenty days they raked the areas of Coy Inlet, different sites of Santa Cruz, Chalí Aike and Cerro Palique, and contacted the Chilean police near Ultima Esperanza. They only found some abandoned horses with an unknown brand in the mouth of the river Coyle.

The pursuers were beginning to feel desperate. They knew they were up against outlaws who had been very clever in planning their escape: plenty of fresh horses; they rode along unknown roads; they avoided the more populated centers; they skirted the *estancias* and stations, misleading them with false clues. Except for Güer Aike, they never found a trace worth following, nothing to encourage them in this fruitless search.

As to the amount of money they stole, there were several different versions: 1) there were more than twenty thousand pesos plus eighty-three pounds sterling inside the metal box -which, by the way, was found four days after the robbery with its lock forced open- 2) There were more than thirty thousand pesos.

The cart driver Francisco Cuello had found the metal box in Manantiales de Killik Aike. He was the man who, at the trio´s request, had transported their supplies to the kitchen of the Sutherland *estancia.* His deposition figures in the police records.

The chief of police, in his presentation before the judge, declared that the outlaws:

> *"...had been preparing their audacious coup for several months, having been seen in Lago Argentino and in Las Horquetas camping*

PATAGONIA

and telling the neighbors that they were looking for land."

In the police records Ethel Place is barely mentioned as "a third party involved, a woman of secondary importance in the robbery".

It was the weekly "*El Antártico*" that mentioned "the third party involved":

> "*The fugitives had left three tired horses at the supply station La Leona, the two that they had been riding and another one...*"

Other references pointed to the presence of a woman when they were pretending to be interested in buying lands; this same woman was seen the day before the robbery, and they guessed she must have gone to the place where the first group of fresh horses was waiting for them.

Then of course they started putting two and two together, such as the shopping they did in Río Gallegos: ammunition for Winchesters, a compass, some binoculars, horseshoes, food stuff and other provisions they needed "because they were going on a lengthy inspection tour of different lands".

Another cart driver said that in Bajada de Urbina "he saw a group of people with several horses, at a distance. They were practicing shooting".

The question was, did the outlaws have fun all the time, or did they at any moment feel harassed by their pursuers? Because the fact is that nothing went wrong. Each detail had been calculated to perfection. They worked out their crime with professional expertise.

During their evenings spent in the Club del Progreso or the Café de Farina, whenever they were chatting with other people, they inquired about the gold prospectors in Tierra del Fuego and some channels in the Straits; was it true that there was a lot of gold and that some people had made a fortune with a mine. Of course, they never seemed terribly interested in the subject. When someone told them that all that was in the past and that at that moment the amount of gold didn´t justify an investment, they quickly changed the subject.

Afterwards, people realized that neither of those two North Americans were particularly interested in digging and working in the ice-cold waters of the river. They were interested in gold, very much indeed, but the kind of gold that has been already processed and coined and kept in a safe. It was much easier to get at.

The police in Río Gallegos had in their hands all the data concerning the outlaws, which had been sent to them by the chief of the Federal Police,

Rosendo Fraga, who had, in turn, received them from the North American Consulate.

Two years before the Río Gallegos bank robbery, the Pinkerton Agency had commissioned detective Frank Dimaio to travel to Buenos Aires and deliver printed documentation, particulars and other data concerning the outlaws, plus the warrant for their arrest. The Pinkerton report had a very detailed account of the gang´s movements and stressed the fact that they were expert riders and even better marksmen.

(The report also mentioned Harvey Logan, who had escaped from Knoxville prison, Tennessee, two years back. But keeping track of the outlaws was no easy task: they were mistakenly looking for Logan in Patagonia, when, in actual fact, he had already committed suicide after the failure of the assault on a train in the Far West).

In Cholila, life stopped being peacefully bucolic for the North Americans. They became suddenly wary; they fortified the cabin… maybe they were trying to imitate their bunker in Brown´s Hole? (Brown´s Hole was the hiding place they had in the Big Horne mountains, Wyoming. Access to it was by way of a narrow mountain pass through a high forty-five- kilometers-long wall of red rock. The hideout was practically on the border of the states of Utah and Colorado. It was the perfect hiding place for the outlaws on account of its distance and because it was inaccessible to outsiders. Their pursuers abandoned the search quickly enough, whilst the bandits could come and go as they pleased without being seen. They knew all the secret places where they could hide stolen cattle, mainly horses).

Although there weren´t so many natural resources to make a stronghold out of their lodge in Cholila, they put their imagination to good use and devised ways and means to build their own "bunker". For example, they installed the yard in such a position that it would intercept any incoming attack, and they took other precautions, such as putting Scandinavian-type windows in the cabin, that could be used in a cross-fire. They also built a tunnel that reached the river, which could eventually allow a quick flight towards what is now lake Lezana, and from there try to disappear in the high mountain forests.

The Pinkerton Agency hoped that this time the outlaws would be trapped. But their desire was not to be fulfilled. In actual fact, they had to admit that the bandits outsmarted them in everything: they were sly and cunning when planning their coups, and they devised all sorts of clever ways to vanish into thin air. The fact of having chosen Río Gallegos as the victim was proof enough. Being so far from Cholila, who could have connected them with the robbery?

But Río Gallegos was chosen on account of its prosperity. Cattle breeding and commerce were in overt expansion; maritime movement became more important due to the activity of the sheep farms. Even though the regular population amounted to nine hundred inhabitants, people spoke in many different languages: English, German, French, Italian and, of course, Spanish, mixed and combined in the characteristic sound of any cosmopolitan center.

There was plenty of money too. Rich landowners eager to buy and spend, and a market full of imported goods to offer. Imported products came mostly from Europe and the U.S.A., and there was very active trading with Punta Arenas.

Cassidy and Sundance concluded that the bank in such a place would certainly not disappoint them.

Some time before, around 1930, when the trio traveled to the Welsh colony of Chubut (Butch Cassidy went first, Sundance and Ethel some months after), they visited Trelew. Following Matthew H. Jones´s references, they contacted the general manager of the Banco Nación, a North American by the name of Howard. According to Jones, the idea was to gather information that would help them plan a robbery in that bank, but nothing came of it. If they ever had the idea of a coup they finally decided against it.

Among the depositions included in the indictment in Río Gallegos there were those of the bank clerks, one of Francisco Cuello the cart driver, and also that of a North American called Santiago Allsop, who worked as a salesman for Little & Co. of London. He seemed a rather dull man and gave very little information, apparently some worthless data that may have been offered him on purpose by Cassidy in order to confuse things.

Once Allsop had become entangled in a lengthy conversation with his dangerous fellow countrymen he gave them very detailed information as to who he was and where he came from, and that his father-in-law, Mr. Vance, had a ranch in Texas. Immediately Cassidy "remembered" having stayed at Mr. Vance´s ranch! Our Mr. Allsop hardly recovered from the surprise, he just clung on to his attaché and left, shaking his head and mumbling in awe "Just wait till I tell my father-in-law!"...

Another coup

Their other big coup was in December of 1905, in the Banco Nación of Villa Mercedes, San Luis, where they introduced themselves as "English landowners" and left richer by fourteen thousand pesos. The manager had tried to resist and was wounded, although not very seriously. It was presumed that Robert "Bob" Evans took part in that robbery. He used to see the trio quite often, and he even spent the night at their place in Cholila.

From Chile they crossed over to San Luis and returned there after the robbery, which meant riding for many days armed with their Winchesters and always on the alert. Rumors were that they were chased by the police and that there was plenty of shooting going on.

In 1904 Bob Evans –who occasionally went by the name of Hood- together with a fellow countryman called Grice who worked in the Compañía Tierras del Sur, in Leleque, were suspected of having robbed five thousand pesos from a steward of that firm. They escaped and, for some time, nobody knew what had become of them.

The North Americans´ peaceful farming period was coming to an end. News of the Río Gallegos robbery had spread and the trio guessed it was time to move on. It seems their good friend Daniel J. Gibbon warned them the police were after them, and that decided them to sell their property and cattle to a chilean firm, for twenty thousand pesos.

All the data about the fugitives plus excerpts of their correspondence figure in a file in the law court of Rawson, Chubut. But in the sales book of the Leleque company, the pages showing entries signed by Cassidy and commercial operations had been torn out.

Sundance wrote to Daniel J. Gibbon informing him of the sale and the twenty thousand pesos they had collected. Actually, there was nothing to be afraid of regarding that sale, because the Chilean company, Cochamó, was most interested in buying Argentine lands near the border. Had Butch and Sundance known the real motive they would have certainly put up the price, as we shall see later on in the episode described by the teacher, Calderón.

Sundance also said in that letter:

> *"I don´t ever want to see Cholila again but I will often think of you and all our friends".*

He also let Gibbon know that he and Ethel would be traveling to San

Francisco, from Chile.

Nevertheless, a few months later Sundance went back to Cholila with Evans, to collect some money that John Comodoro Perry owed them for the sale of some horses and sheep that he had carried out in Daniel Gibbon´s name. That was the last time Sundance Kid was in Argentina; he returned to Chile and then went to Bolivia. On the other hand, Bob "Hood" Evans went back to Cholila.

Ethel stayed in U.S.A. and Sundance returned to join Cassidy. Both would then enter the last stage of their adventures in South America: Bolivia.

According to police information, Butch Cassidy was by then forty years old, Sundance was 39 and Etta:

> "27 or 28, 1,65 m. tall, weight around 50 kilos. Thin, white skin, auburn hair and greenish eyes".

Cassidy measured

> "1,75 m., fair hair, strong jaws, two scars in the back of his head, another very small one under left eye, and a small mole on one of his ankles".

This was Sundance´s description:

> "Swedish-American, sturdy, healthy-white (?) color skin, with reddish-brown beard or moustache, blue eyes and a longish nose; greek-style features; usually combs with great care".

This description included a word of warning: "All these people, including the woman, are excellent shooters with firearms". But the warning was no longer useful because Ethel was back in the U.S.A., and Cassidy and Sundance had been lured by a country that promised them generous mines full of precious metals and banks loaded with money. They both traveled a long way to the mining district.

As for Ethel, rumors had it that she traveled to Denver to have an appendix operation, others said that the appendix was really a pregnancy due to an infidelity with a farmer in Esquel. Anyway, it was just gossip...

An uncertain end

In Bolivia, Butch Cassidy and Sundance worked for a fellow countryman called Michael Siebert, in a tin mine, "Concordia". That´s as far as the actual facts go. From then on, the only news of their whereabouts was a messy report by Arthur Chapman, a serial writer who specialized in the Far West, and who wrote in the *Elk´ Magazine* the sort of fiction that serial readers love.

Many years later, the film about the outlaws based on the script written by Goldman gave a definite end to their story, ignoring many episodes that really took place during the six years that elapsed between their departure from the U.S.A. and their arrival in Bolivia.

Many books have been written about Cassidy, each one giving a different version. The serial writers Dora Flak and Larry Pointer maintain that Cassidy and Sundance lived to a ripe old age. Allan Swallow, in *"The Wild Bunch"*, tends to stick to actual facts. Lula Parker Betenson, in *"Butch Cassidy, my brother"*, insisted that she met her brother Butch, in 1925, and they both had tea with raspberry pie. But, undoubtedly, one of the most reliable accounts was that of Kerry Ross Boren, a historian of the outlaws of Manila, Ohio.

And, as for William Goldman, even though he carried out valuable research on the subject, the script he wrote was more in keeping with the demands of the movie industry, where facts can be twisted around and truth is distorted in the name of entertainment.

Some writers agree with Chapman in that both died in Bolivia in 1908 or 1909. Others sustain that they met their death in an encounter with the Uruguayan police (rumors had it that this version was planted by the Pinkerton Agency which was eager to have them "killed" one way or another).

And as for Ethel, reports state that she was last seen in Denver in 1925.

Among all these different versions, the most popular with the highest degree of credibility was that Butch Cassidy –under the alias William K. Phillips- spent his last years in Spokane, Washington, where he died in 1937. And as for Sundance Kid, it was rumored that he went back to Ethel and that they lived together until he died, in 1946, and was buried in Casper, Wyoming. This version was reaffirmed when the alleged graves of the two outlaws in Bolivia were opened, in 1992. The bones were sent to the U.S.A. for a forensic study. The result was negative.

What most writers coincide on is the date of both men´s disappearance, which is 1911. The time had come to give them up for dead. It did their pursuers no favor to keep them alive after almost two decades of chasing these criminals that humiliated them once and again.

PATAGONIA

There were many versions about the end of Butch Cassidy and Sundance Kid. Maybe one of them is true. But...which one?

An unfulfilled desire

Twice, Butch Cassidy felt a yearning desire to settle down –on a permanent basis- as a respectable stock farmer. The first was in Cholila, Argentina; the second, in Santa Cruz de la Sierra, Bolivia. However, that did not form part of Sundance´s plans and maybe that explains why Butch was unable to carry out his project. His relationship with Sundance was stronger than a contradiction he carried throughout his life, which was that, much as he hated his roots as a puritan farmer because of the miserable way of life it entailed, they also instilled in him a deep devotion for the land.

Although Butch stood out as the most mature of the two, in the end he always gave in to Sundance´s impulses. Sundance seemed to find the meaning of life in crime and leading an intense and dissolute existence.

After living four years in Cholila, Cassidy was already adjusting to his role as a farmer. But it was hard on Sundance and Ethel, who craved for excitement and hated their monotonous, irrelevant life there. And that marked the end of the farming experience.

In Bolivia it was even less probable to make his dream come true because Ethel had already returned to the U.S.A.. Cassidy was then left alone with his unfulfilled desire, and the impulsive recklessness of his partner. Now that Ethel was gone, the two grew closer to each other than ever before.

Cassidy declared he had found "the" place he had previously imagined when he was nearing 35, in Patagonia, and at the age of 41, in Bolivia. But he never managed to settle down...

Maybe that is the reason why he always had, at the back of his mind, a Scottish legend that intrigued him: the story about John Mac Donald of the Isles, founder of the clan bearing his name, and who ran in a racing competition by sea for the possession of an island. The first of the competitors to arrive would win its ownership.

The sea was rough and the race was hard-going. When John realized he could be left behind, he tried to calculate the distance to the island, and then promptly cut off his left arm and hurled it with vehemence onto the island.

That was his terrible way of getting there first.

This bloody incident was always present in Cassidy´s mind, as a symbol of the extremes a man can go to when he is driven by the obsession of owning his land.

And yet, throughout his life, Cassidy was always an errant soul, always on the move. He was a runaway, that was the style that shaped his existence.

Wilson and Evans

After Butch Cassidy and Sundance´s disappearance, another couple of outlaws entered the scene. Their names: Bob Evans and William Wilson, whose identities were often mistaken for those of Cassidy and Sundance.

But when one analyzes their uncouth behavior and brutal ways it becomes quite obvious that they have nothing in common with the previous outlaws. Other minor criminals also intervened, but in brief and isolated appearances.

Since 1875 quite a few cowboys had come from the Far West to settle down in the North of Argentina. Even though they were skilled workers, they were looked down upon with a certain degree of distrust, especially in the north of the province of Santa Fe, where they had founded the colonies California and Alejandra (the latter was founded in collaboration with Swiss immigrants).

The North Americans –William and Ben Moore, Simpson, Bayley, Taylor, Mac Lean, Colman, Nelson, Spencer, Griffin, Fortshire, Chapman, Pogh, Fort- from the California colony, and others from Alejandra, joined forces in an expedition that raided the Indian camp of Malabrigo, because, or so they said, the Indians had stolen horses, killed two colonists and taken two children captive.

On their return, they burnt down and attacked other camps they found on their way, killing in revenge all the native men, women and children they happened to see during that two-hundred-and-fifty-kilometer-long march.

Perhaps it was their way of recreating the old Far West.

As we already mentioned, Bob Evans returned to Cholila from Chile, after Sundance left for Bolivia. He devoted his time to searching for gold, and some time later was joined by Richard Perkins, who was the son of a North

American that was working under contract for the railroad in Córdoba.

In September 1911, the newspaper *"La Nación"* published an interview with the "North American outlaw Perkins", who was taken prisoner in the Federal Capital for having taken part in the frustrated robbery of Casa Lahusen, in Comodoro Rivadavia.

He had been a civil servant in the Pacífico Railroad and –unbelievably– had graduated as a lieutenant from the aristocratic Military School in Richmond, Virginia, capital city of the Confederates during the Civil War.

Once he gave up his job in the railroad he traveled to the Cordillera where he eventually got a job as an accountant in the Compañía Tierras del Sur, in Leleque.

Perkins denied having established a relationship with the North American gunmen other than could be expected of a neighbor. He also said that "Place and Ryan (alias Sundance and Cassidy) had many friends".

The Governor in person had been a guest in their house, the police respected them and their neighbors had a high opinion of them, so what was wrong about being friendly with them?

The search for gold ended in a complete failure. Evans and Perkins decided to leave Tierra del Fuego and, on their return trip, stopped at Comodoro Rivadavia.

As a way of making up for this frustration they planned to rob the establishment of Christian Lahusen, who traded in wool, hides and rural equipment. For this coup they counted on the help of the Chilean *peón* who worked for Perkins.

But the *peón* was not too pleased with his share of the booty and rebelled against his employer and his partner. They were so offended by this *peón's* insolence that one of them shot him. Some witnesses blamed Evans for the shooting of the Chilean, others thought Perkins was responsible. Perkins returned to Cholila and, with the Gibbons's help, left the Cordillera. A warrant for his arrest was issued and, three years later, he was taken prisoner in Buenos Aires.

Perkins told his side of the story and explained that he and his friend's purpose was to carry out "exchange operations", and they did not, by any means, intend to rob the establishment. And when they were about to return to the Cordillera, the *peón* hired by Evans rebelled, which infuriated his employer and drove him to shoot him, twice. Perkins, on the other hand, stated that he saw the *peón* run away, and therefore gathered he hadn´t been wounded. He found out much later that he had died.

His testimony in Buenos Aires must have been very convincing, because he got off scot-free, thanks to –how could it be otherwise!- the help provided by certain valuable contacts.

Some time later, Bob Evans joined up with the Texan William Wilson, who reached Esquel on 1908 after leaving General Villegas, where he lived with his brother since he arrived in Argentina, in 1904. Roaming around the district was another fellow countryman called Peter Litjens, who had worked as a cowboy in Santa Fe and Entre Ríos. He was a friend of Andrew Duffy, who was mistakenly taken for Harvey Logan by many people. But, the fact was that Logan had been buried four years ago, and his tomb was covered with weeds. Andrew Duffy had taken part in many robberies in the Far West with different gangs, with "Black" Jack Ketchum, Henry Ieuch and Harry Tracy, the killer. His homicidal urge was so devastating that Evans and Mansel Gibbon were "obliged" to shoot him in order to get him out of the way. Duffy´s death was described by Wenceslao Solís, a *peón* that Cassidy and Sundance had in high esteem, and who later moved out to Río Pico.

Evans´s and Wilson´s activity was buying and selling cattle. And every now and then, they stole horses. Until one day it occurred to Wilson that there were better –and quicker- ways of getting hold of some ready cash.

William Wilson was informed of the date when an important sum of money was due at the Compañía Mercantil, in Arroyo Pescado, to pay for the wool after sheep shearing. They were on the lookout, and when the stagecoach that they thought was bringing the money arrived, they went into the shop. Of course they were well-known there as clients, they often bought fishing gear. So the manager, an engineer called Llwyd Ap Iwan, was more than surprised when he saw the muzzle of a 45 Mauser in his face and was ordered to open the safe. He assured them that there were not more than fifty pesos in the safe but the thieves thought he was lying and obliged him to open it up.

Although Ap Iwan had one of his hands bandaged, he thought he had enough time to knock Wilson down and disarm him…. But the North American shot him straight in the heart, and the Welshman died instantly. One of the clerks revealed that a shot was heard in Ap Iwan´s office, and then two more. The manager had tried to snatch the weapon from Wilson, and in the ensuing struggle, a shot was fired accidentally. So then the outlaw got hold of a small revolver he kept hidden in a pocket and shot the Welshman several times.

This outrageous crime brought about rightful indignation among the settlers because the victim was a prominent member of the Welsh community. The engineer Llwyd Ap Iwan had carried out important tasks as a land surveyor, geographer and explorer, all of which resulted in contributions of great value not only for the Welsh colony but for the country as well.

His discovery of the river Fénix, in Santa Cruz, would later reinforce the arguments used by the "Perito" Moreno in the borders conflict with Chile.

A couple of days later (nobody can find an explanation for this delay) three groups commanded by Milton Roberts, Daniel Harrington and Daniel Gibbon respectively, left in search of the outlaws who had already run off towards the South-East, to Río Pico, where they had a hideout. According to one version, once Milton Roberts had found the runaways´ hiding place, he returned to request Harrington´s and Gibbon´s participation. As Gibbon, together with his sons, had a record that didn´t quite place him on the right side of the law, he tried to persuade the members of the other two committees to drop the persecution because –in Milton Roberts´s words- "the North Americans would kill them like dogs". They were his friends after all…

Some months later the police superintendent Eduardo Humphreys received several prisoners sent to him by the chief inspector Narciso Espinosa; among them were Daniel Gibbon in person, his sons Mansel and Tomás, Peter Litjens and Andrew Duffy. Apparently Andrew Duffy managed to smuggle a weapon into his cell, which he later used to escape, together with Mansel Gibbon. They both went to Río Pico, to Wilson and Evans´s hideout, and went back to their favorite activity, which was stealing cattle and then selling it in Chile.

It is hard to understand how Daniel Gibbon (dear friend of Cassidy and Sundance and sometimes their front man) and his sons weren´t overtly rejected by the community. But in those days, according to T. Caillet Bois "felony and crime were everyday things and the few honorable men were terrified". Maybe that explanation can shed some light.

Another episode in the lives of Evans and Wilson had Lucio Ramos Otero as main character.

This young man belonged to a family of *estancieros* of the province of Buenos Aires. Nobody really knows why he ever appeared in Patagonia: was it because he had an urge for adventure like so many youths of his age?, or maybe because he wanted to get away from a world full of formality, or because he liked to be on his own or was he psychologically unstable? He may also have been under the influence of some writings where adventure gave meaning to the existence of those who felt trapped in a world made up of stale traditional codes.

Ramos Otero was part of a team of engineers and surveyors led by the French naturalist Henri de la Veaux, who traveled to Patagonia to carry out topographic surveys. Only Ramos Otero went as a cook...

After several weeks of not collecting their wages, the *peones* started to demand their money in unpleasant terms. In despair, the head of the committee vainly tried to explain that funds sent from Buenos Aires would arrive any moment. But his surprise knew no bounds when the young cook, whose appearance had always seemed out of keeping with his job, offered to advance the men´s pay out of his own money: "When the money from Buenos Aires arrives you can pay me back". And, to everybody´s amazement, he started to get wads of money out of his pockets. Once his true identity became known there was a logical explanation for his looks, his manners and his clothes which, although worn, were obviously of good quality and taste.

Asencio Abeijón tells that, some time after, Lucio traveled to the Cordillera, where he worked as a *peón* for an engineer that measured lands, and who dismissed him after a rather strange episode. In one of the engineer´s trips to Buenos Aires, Ramos Otero asked him to post a letter for his mother, in any post office in Buenos Aires. But the engineer decided to take it personally, and when he got to the address, he found himself facing an elegant mansion. He immediately thought this lad´s mother must be one of the servants and delivered the letter to the butler, who, when reading what was written on the envelope, asked the engineer to wait a moment. Finally he was led into a beautifully furnished hall where a very well-dressed lady asked, with tears in her eyes, about Lucio.

When the letter-bearer returned, he dismissed young Ramos Otero without any apparent reason. Maybe he thought it improper to have a person of his social standing working as a rural laborer.

Shortly after, Lucio Ramos Otero bought an *estancia* in Corcovado, and all these stories spread like wildfire among the villagers who, in turn, must have distorted them to make them even more exciting. Ah, well, poetic justice… In any event, Wilson and Evans also heard these eccentric anecdotes and thought this crazy *estanciero* would be a perfect victim.

On the last day of March 1911, in a site known as Cañadón del Tiro, Wilson and Evans intercepted the cart which Ramos Otero used for traveling, together with his *peón* José Quintanilla. They were obliged to follow them, first to their *estancia*, where they stole money and other objects of value, and then to the outlaws' hideout in the mountains.

Apparently this was a kidnapping for which they believed they could get a generous ransom.

The captors obliged Ramos Otero to write a letter to his mother telling her that they would set him free if she paid the ransom of one hundred and twenty thousand pounds. Otherwise, he guessed they would kill him.

His imprisonment lasted for twenty six days: Ramos Otero and his *peón* were both scared and depressed. Nevertheless, he made the most of the opportunity when one of the guards dropped a match on the ground. Ramos Otero kept the match and used it later to build a fire and burn the strips of leather that held the wooden poles of the improvised prison together. That night, both prisoners were able to escape.

When Wilson and Evans discovered the prisoners had escaped, they went after them. Helping them were their accomplices, a Chilean called Juan Vidal, and Mansel Gibbon who, according to Ramos Otero, was the most vulgar of the bunch.

The first thing Ramos Otero did was go to his neighbor's house. The lady in question, Rosalba Solís, was dismayed at the sight of this young man who was stammering and trembling at her door, obviously in a state of shock. And she was downright scared when some rough and threatening gunmen appeared a few hours afterwards looking for the runaway. They ransacked her house and then left, after making sure that he was not hiding there.

Lucio Ramos Otero continued feeling worried. Two of his brothers had come from Buenos Aires with the ransom money demanded, but he said all this was a farce, a put up job because the kidnapping had been his family's idea to oblige him to return home.

The police weren't too convinced with his story and only began to take him seriously when Lucio led them to the hideout where he had been kept prisoner. Of course it was too late to capture the outlaws, they had already left some time back.

The North Americans had gone down to Río Pico to buy bandages and remedies and have Wilson´s hand seen to -a cartridge had exploded in his right hand-. Two brothers, Eduardo and Juan Hahn, approached them and warned them the police were after them so they had to get away quickly. Guillermina Hahn cleaned the wound and fixed it up. They got some provisions and went back to their hiding place.

A police patrol led by the Second Lieutenant Jesús Blanco and Police Inspector Eufemio Palleres went after the outlaws. Apparently, they were held responsible for Ramos Otero´s kidnapping and the killing of Ap Iwan. Wilson and Evans were mentioned

> "...in complicity with Mansel Gibbon, 24 year-old, Argentinian, and the Chileans Wenceslao Solís, Juan, Diego, Guillermo and Eusebio Cadagan, who helped them".

Once the brothers Solís and Cadagan were under arrest, the border police commission continued an inch-by-inch scrutiny of the river until they reached the hill Botella Oeste, which was the place where Ramos Otero had been held captive after the kidnapping. They visited Claudio Solís´s place and then continued up to Juan Holessen´s home. They questioned him about the criminals and Holessen said that "a few days ago he had seen the camp´s canvas at approximately one league's distance". Second Lieutenant Blanco obliged him to show him the way, and ordered his men to have their rifles at hand, ready to fire.

In the police report, Blanco stated that Robert Evans and William Wilson opened fire but, according to some neighbors present, that wasn´t altogether true. Besides, the frontier police were well-known for shooting first and then taking a look.

Always according to Blanco´s report, the policemen advanced

> "...at such speed that Roberto Evans, who had already spent all his ammunition and had no time to load his gun, wounded soldier Urbano Montenegro in the chest with his last shot and then left his Winchester to one side and grabbed his 45 Mauser, fired a few shots but was then wounded by some of the men under my orders.
> Soldier Cándido Ríos, aware that Evans continued shooting and had managed to wound soldier Pedro Peña in his right arm, shot

the bandit right in the middle of his chest and killed him.
In the meantime, William Wilson, taking cover in the forest and the
secret places afforded by mountainous ground, managed to get
away. He threw his Winchester in the bushes and took off one of his
boots to run faster. But soldier Pedro Rojas was chasing him on
horseback and finally caught up with him. He shot him while riding
and missed. So he dismounted to face the bandit who was pointing
his gun at him, and soldier Rojas triggered first. Wilson dropped to
the ground with two bullets lodged in his chest".

The persecution lasted for over a year. During that period, the police had
several encounters with Wilson´s gang that threw no positive results. Ramos
Otero disliked the border police, and, in his opinion, the police were so afraid
of the bandits that they used to shoot prematurely.

The indictment doesn´t mention Mansel Gibbon nor the Chilean Juan
Vidal. They also formed part of the gang, but they got away and managed to
cross the border. Several neighbors confirmed having seen Gibbon in 1922,
but he quickly returned to Chile and was never heard of since.

Soldier Montenegro died a few minutes after having been shot. Pedro
Peña was wounded in an arm, taken to Eduardo Hahn´s house for first aid care
of the wound and then sent to Tecka.

Montenegro´s wake was held in this German settler´s house, and, in
Lieutenant Blanco´s report:

"I beckoned all the neighbors living within five leagues´ distance
from Eduardo Hahn´s house and had the two outlaws´ dead bodies
identified. They were unanimously recognized as the North
Americans Roberto Evans and William Wilson. A report was drawn
up and signed by the residents Juan Holessen, Emilio Hermann,
Juan B. Munita, Belisario Contreras, Ernesto Stann, Claudio Solís,
Martín Erath and Juan Hahn.
After the formalities I had the dead bodies buried about a block
away from Eduardo Hahn´s house".

Constantino Salinas Jaca, a respected inhabitant of the district, had a
different version:

"Evans was seasoning a stew, while Wilson was lying down; his
right hand was very inflamed. Maybe he was asleep, and the border
police had no difficulty in approaching them without being seen.

Lieutenant Blanco ordered "Fire!" and Evans dropped to the ground, dead. Quick as a flash, Wilson was able to get hold of a gun and shoot while running away; he killed one of his pursuers and wounded another. In any case, Wilson realized he was lost and, knowing what was in store for him if he fell into the hands of the border police, he chose to commit suicide".

Several days went by before Wilson and Evans were buried. Time enough to take pictures and finish writing a bulky report which could prove, without a shade of doubt, the identity of the dead bodies. Obviously, the forty thousand pesos offered for the capture of the bandits demanded a thorough job...

Continuing with Salinas Jaca's report:

"The police had finished and done with the report and yet they didn't bother to bury the lifeless bodies. I am certain these were abandoned in the esplanade of the only commerce of the district and that it was the owners of the premises, Messrs. Hahn who, in view of such outrageous abandonment, took upon themselves the charitable and merciful mission of digging the grave where the weary bodies of Evans and Wilson would finally find eternal rest.

Salinas Jaca was of the opinion that the Hahn brothers honored the Christian principle according to which one must hate sin and be merciful with the sinner.

Also figuring in the report was the fact that "among the outlaws's belongings there was a magazine, *"The Wide World Magazine"*, published in September 1910, nobody knows how they got it". Maybe the outlaws were interested in an article signed by John Mc Intosh, a frustrated detective who took up writing police stories of the Far West. In what would be his first, and also last investigation, the Pinkerton Agency had sent him to Chinook, Montana, to capture Kid Curry (Harvey Logan), author of many crimes.

Apparently, Mc Intosh traveled pretending to be a soap salesman. He descended from the train and stayed at the only hotel in town. He was reading the papers and having a drink. Suddenly, he saw two men sitting at another table making signs at him, inviting him to join them. He tried to avoid them but the men were most insistent, which made him feel very uneasy.

The following day he went into a shop to offer his soaps and was amazed when the shop-keeper said to him:

- You may be very good, but your looks are against you. Word's got around that you are trying to take Curry to trial, but he never molested anybody around here... You may not be a detective, but Curry's friends think otherwise. I don't care who you are, stranger. Butch Cassidy sent word that you have an hour to leave this town.

John Mc Intosh looked at his watch. It was 11 a.m. And he smiled, relieved because he was still in time to board the North Express that stopped there at 11.45 sharp.

On his return, he acknowledged feeling frustrated, humiliated and...glad to be still alive. He was also right on time to present his resignation to the Pinkerton Agency.

Mc Intosh's version -which appeared in the *Wide World Magazine* found in Río Pico- was rather strange, even though he maintained that it was based on documentation that was all in the Archives of the National Bureau of Criminal Identification of the U.S.A.:

"The State Department received a cable from the Consul accredited in Buenos Aires informing that the Wild Bunch operated in Argentina. In view of this country's impossibility of cornering them, it requests help in order to get rid of the predators".

One week later, five detectives from different States of the Union –who for safety measures omitted mentioning their names- traveled to Argentina. Sponsors of this operation were the National Bankers' Association, the Pinkerton National Detective Agency, the three railway companies of the West and major J. Silvester, head of the International Association of Chiefs of Police.

This police mission arrived when the *ménage à trois* living in Cholila were on their best behavior. In any case, getting to the "precordillera" was a bold, risky operation.

The Border Police

The Border Police was created in 1910 during the presidency of Sáenz Peña. It was called the Foreign Legion because it assembled men of different origins and nationalities, many of them with doubtful records. There were Spaniards, Italians, Russians, Portuguese, French, Africans, Uruguayans, Brazilians, Paraguayans and Argentines. They were ruthless men, excellent riders and experts in the use of sabers and rifles.

Their chiefs were Major Mateo Gebhard in Chubut and Major Adrián del Busto, in Río Negro. The forces assigned to Chubut were, by far, the most relevant, due to Gebhard´s imposing personality and the importance of his undertakings.

Gebhard was born in Prague. When he was twenty years old he was a midshipman on a German warship. During one of the ship´s voyages it stopped at Punta Arenas, and Gebhard deserted, having previously punched an officer in the face. He dove into the ice-cold sea water and escaped swimming. Since then he roamed throughout Patagonia working in whatever job he could get. Most of the time he worked as a shepherd. He joined the Argentine Army as a sergeant and, some time later, was assigned by the Ministry of the Interior to organize the Border Police.

He pursued many gunmen. But, by far the most famous manhunt was that of Wilson and Evans. He also harassed many Chilean outlaws, and he succeeded in capturing José Pozzi, famous for his brutal crimes. Pozzi and his gang had assaulted the family of a settler called William Thomas, and also a store next to the river Percy belonging to an Italian merchant.

Gebhard and his party had managed to kill the criminal´s horse, but they couldn´t catch Pozzi, who ran desperately towards the border. Gebhard let his men follow the route they had taken, but he himself made a detour to intercept him.

He described future events as follows:

> *"There was a broadside of shots thundering in the ravine. The blast was so deafening I thought it came from the guns of the Chilean infantry. I didn´t imagine it came from my own people´s rifles. I raced towards the river. It was dark and I fell from the frost-covered edge of the gorge. Another blast shook the mountains and the bullets pierced the ground all around me but I can assure you I was overjoyed because now I was certain it was my men who had shot the first broadside and that it was practically impossible for Pozzi to escape. We found him at dawn. Two bullets had perforated his body, another two had destroyed his thighs and he had remained during all that winter night in the river waters. He didn´t utter a word when we carried him to the river bank, and he didn´t answer our questions. I said to him:*
> *- You have only twenty minutes to live; enough to save your soul.*

PATAGONIA

Tell me who are your accomplices —Pozzi didn´t answer-
- You´re dying…
- I don´t give a damn…

Some of the Frontier policemen were not very subtle when it came down to establishing a difference between friends or foes. Once, a group that was after the Chilean outlaw Basilio Possa and shot him down together with other members of the gang, afterwards chased the survivors who escaped to Esquel through the mountains, towards a gorge that was later called Cañadón de los Bandidos. Going with them as a scout was Fortunato Fernández, a shepherd of the Compañía de Tierras del Sur de Leleque.

Chief Dreyer, in charge of the group, ordered his men to line up in single file to get across a narrow pass. In the meantime, the scout had to go on ahead to follow the trail. Suddenly, out of the blue and without previous warning, some policemen started to shoot because they saw, just ahead of them, the silhouette of a man crouching. After shooting him they ran away, presuming him —the alleged outlaw- to be dead.

The following day a villager, Eduardo Humphreys, an ex Police Inspector, found the person who had been shot by the Border police. He was no other than Fernández the scout, who was lying on the floor, moaning, in a puddle of blood. Humphreys took him to Esquel, where he had one of his legs cut off, and had his wounds cleaned and cared for.

Bailey Willis, the famous North American geologist, had nothing but praise for Gebhard´s expert performance in capturing criminals. He reported a conversation he once had with Gebhard about a certain character called Pierre Vergon "a mysterious Frenchman whose culture, refinement and subtle power make his presence in Esquel a sort of enigma".

-Very dangerous man —replied Gebhard- . A real criminal; I only wish I could get his fingerprints.

The major had no definite proof. It was just a hunch.

He was most upset when he saw the prisoners returning from Rawson free of blame and charges. He thereupon decided he would not send to trial any man that his instinct believed was guilty. He implanted the "law of escape", and there were several feigned escapes that ended up in virtual executions.

Asencio Abeijón reported a case which shows the peculiarity of certain procedures. A muleteer from Buenos Aires had run away from a police inspector who tried to arrest him for hunting in private property without a permit. He decided to try his luck in Patagonia. After becoming involved in several brawls over gambling or over wages which were less than had been previously agreed upon, or over debts, etc. etc., he decided to become a policeman.

He not only received a handsome uniform, he was also presented with a magnificent horse that had belonged to an Englishman who, together with his wife and children, had been murdered. According to Abeijón, the killer slaughtered the couple´s two small children "because he couldn´t bear the thought of leaving two abandoned orphans". This abominable character escaped to Chile and, when he was crossing the border, came face to face with two *carabineros* who were taking a criminal prisoner.

He introduced himself as an Argentine citizen, spent the night in the police camp and the following morning, while they were rolling up their rugs, shot them in the back and set the prisoner free. Together they returned to Chubut and murdered a cattleman, robbing him of the money obtained in a cattle sale they had witnessed.

Sarmiento´s Police Inspector said to his new subordinate:
- *"Go after him and bring him to me, no matter how, just bring him to me"*.

The new policeman knew he could cope, he was a good shot.

He traced the fugitives –by that time they were three- and discovered them resting beside a brook. He calculated that maybe he couldn´t deal with them on his own, so he went to the nearest Chilean frontier post and asked for help. The Chileans were anxious to take revenge on the man who had murdered the *carabineros* and were only too pleased to appoint a couple of expert scouts to accompany him.

They took the bandits by surprise and, after a brief and intense shooting, the police finally killed two of the murderer´s henchmen. He gave himself up, hoping he might have the opportunity to escape during the long journey to the prison. Besides, he never left witnesses alive. That way, nobody could tell the story, and his crimes were very difficult to prove. He had money enough to hire good lawyers and pay substantial gratuities which, in this particular case, were refused by the police. So he had to consider a different strategy; well, he could say he was a victim of abuse, or complain alleging territorial violation, undue arrest, abuse of authority....

The Argentine policeman, who still thought more in terms of an outlaw than as an officer of the law and supposed that with money and fishy legal maneuvers the criminal could get away with it, became suddenly aware of the height, the precipice, etc. He remarked to the Chileans that no matter what side of the border he was on, the mere mention of territorial violation could create an uncomfortable situation and even block the trial he deserved. The Chileans couldn't agree more, and supported his suggestion. The criminal's bones ended up at the bottom of the precipice.

> - *"Are you absolutely sure?" –the chief inspector insisted-.*
>
> - *"Yes, sir" –answered the young, new officer who had made such an impressive debut.*
>
> - *"I take your word for it but, if he's still around and alive, I will kill him personally and then we talk".*

The Border Police had their camp in Súnica, about fifty kilometers from Esquel. That's where Bailey Willis met Second Lieutenant Blanco, who had been removed from office but worked for Gebhard as secretary. His dismissal was because he stole some sheep from the police storehouse.

Bailey Willis described him as:

> *"very standard among certain circles of the Argentine youth: plump and unscrupulous. The governor of Chubut had him under surveillance and very soon put him under arrest for stealing sheep. There was sufficient proof to back the charges and Blanco was removed from office after serving a short period of time in jail".*

(Chief Inspector Eufemio Palleres, the other leader of the posse that confronted Wilson and Evans, was shot one evening in front of his own house. He was returning home with his wife, Delfina Blanco, teacher at Epuyén, and, when they were getting off the *sulky* they were both murdered by a couple of Chilean bandits hiding in the bushes).

There was a drill in honor of Willis and then Gebhard presented him with the relevant files and documents. After *siesta* (afternoon nap which is customary in many provinces of Argentina) they discussed "the military arrangements that were necessary for the protection of the forests whenever the Argentines decided to banish Chilean intruders from the area".

Most of the bandits were Chilean and, thanks to Gebhard's tenacious pursuit they were obliged to return to their country.

Gebhard´s police force was criticized for its abusive methods, mostly due to its members´ ignorance and excessive power. In some cases their actions were motivated by sheer personal revenge (there were quite a few thieves among them). But, at the same time, they also received the community´s acknowledgement for having eliminated delinquency in the "wild west" of Chubut .

The local authorities loathed Gebhard, who was only answerable to the Minister of the Interior. When referring to the Territory´s Governor, Gebhard admitted that:

> *"...he does all he can to destroy us and tried to have me transferred to another place; but, as he didn´t get away with it, he does his best to molest my officers; one has been dismissed (Jesús Blanco) and two are in jail".*

In 1918, faced by the territorial authorities´ repeated claims and the pressure exerted by certain congressmen –Gebhard had already retired- President Hipólito Yrigoyen finally decided to dissolve the controversial Border Police.

The adventures of Helen Greenhill Beckar

A very strange case indeed, that of an Englishwoman called Helen Greenhill Beckar. Out here she was called "La Inglesa", or "La Grenil". She was born in Yorkshire, England, in the year 1875 and emigrated to Chile when she was fifteen years old, together with her parents, Francis Emma Beckar and John Alfred Greenhill. Apparently her father was a farmer in a place near Victoria, in Chile.

The jurist Alejandro Godoy had access to the police report of this tall, thin, fair-haired bandit and revealed many details of her adventurous life in his story, *"La Matrera"*.

She wore black *bombachas* (a type of baggy trousers) and knee-high boots with Chilean spurs, a vest and a "poncho de Castilla" (a long black cloak made of hand-woven wool, very warm and water-proof. This garment was worn by herdsmen in the Cordillera). A wide-brimmed hat and a chin strap completed her outfit which was, putting it mildly, most surprising. Especially when her long, fair curls escaped from under her hat and spilled on her shoulders.

Elías Chucair, a story-teller from Río Negro, described her as someone who tried to hide the fact that she was a woman. She also tried to conceal her "slender figure, using men´s clothes, generally made of leather. She wore breeches and high boots".

Of course, her adventures were embellished by all sorts of legends and anecdotes which were closer to popular imagination than true facts. But there are also stories based on facts, and data that confirm many episodes of her adventurous existence.

When she was still living in Chile she married a man twenty years her senior, called Manuel de la Cruz Astete. He was a merchant and traveled frequently to Patagonia, mainly to Viedma, Patagones and other towns in Río Negro. By 1898 the married couple had settled in Chelforó, and soon Armando was born. Two years after that they moved to General Roca, where César Eulogio was born.

Shortly after, Manuel de la Cruz Astete was arrested and accused of having robbed a bull in a Chilean *hacienda*. In 1904 they settled down in Corral de Piedra, in Neuquén. The chief of police of that place declared having found the dead body of a man of around fifty years of age. Apparently he had been beaten to death.

It was the body of Cruz Astete.

Eight months later the Justice of the Peace of Catán Lil confirmed the marriage of the thirty-year-old "widow" Elena Greenhill to Martín Coria, aged thirty-four. The newly-married wife declared having been married in Chile to a man whose death was registered in that same law court. Chief inspector José Belindo López was witness to the marriage. Elena Greenhill´s new husband was the son of a farmer in Patagones, an educated man who was on friendly terms with many influential personalities.

So, of course, nobody had any doubts that Cruz Astete´s murderers were none other than his widow and her new husband. But other versions pointed to Coria as the killer.

As main suspects of the murder of Cruz Astete, the newlyweds were harassed by the police. Once they were "visited" by a committee that was sent especially from Chubut to arrest them on the grounds of cattle robbery. Seemingly Coria had convinced a widow, Mercedes Sifuentes de Jara, to sign a power of attorney and he then took her cattle, sold it and kept all the money.

When the police went to arrest Elena during Coria's absence, she managed to disarm the chief of police with one nice, neat shot. All the officers ran away except two who were held "captive" by the Englishwoman and, as punishment, were obliged to do the household chores. Watching over them were two of the three members of the gang who, to add to the amusement, were dressed in the officers' uniforms.

Thanks to the services rendered by the officers, the humble house built on fiscal lands of Monón-Niló was spotless!

On another occasion Elena Greenhill was chatting with a neighbor and having *mates* that were prepared by the *peón*, a deaf-and-dumb Indian. Coria and his henchmen were in another room, engrossed in their own particular chit-chat. Suddenly they heard someone roar:

- Nobody move!

A posse commanded by the Chief of Police of Telsen, Domingo Caligaris, together with a couple of farmers who had been robbed by Coria and his gang, and widow Jara's brother, had the house surrounded. Immediately the gang fired a broadside and the ensuing shooting lasted until the police ran out of ammunition. The neighbor afterwards tried to justify herself saying that they had obliged her to shoot.

When the shooting stopped, the Corias sent the *peón* over with a message. Chief Caligaris and his aide entered the house to hold a parley and were kept as virtual hostages until the following morning.

Coria immediately went over to the police station at Cuy, and reported he had been a "victim of abusive behavior". He accused the police of massive shooting after giving the order "Nobody move!" and that they had therefore been obliged to fire back in order to defend the children (two of his and three of the neighbors). In other words, abuse of authority. And that besides everything was perfectly in order because they had shown Chief Caligaris all the legal documents he demanded, after which the chief and his aide stayed on at his house all night long, drinking. Actually, they left at dawn (It appears the policeman had been "persuaded" to sign the papers at the point of a gun).

The cheek and impudence of this couple knew no limits. They and their gang used to "call on" the cattle-breeders and, with an arrogant display of gun-power, leave the ranch taking away all the cattle.

Martín Coria was taken ill and had to travel to Buenos Aires for medical treatment. In October of 1914 Helen Greenhill was notified of her husband's death. He was forty-three years old, and they had been married nine years.

Except for the fact that Helen Greenhill didn't go in for buying cattle -or anything else for that matter- she considered herself a rancher. She had been a witness to the suspicious way ranchers had of expanding their properties or of unobtrusively mixing alien cattle with their own. So, in a way, she was a sort of imitator.

She was interested in cattle, and she was also keen on men. She couldn't do without them, and a few months after Coria's death she joined up with Martín Taborda.

She had sent her children to Buenos Aires. Armando was already eighteen years old and César Eulogio was sixteen. Meanwhile, she and Taborda traveled to Chubut. Apparently they were going to buy some land. She decided to overlook the fact that she was "wanted". Both the police who she had abducted and humiliated and the ranchers that had been robbed by her were eagerly waiting, ready to pounce and lay their hands on the lady.

According to a neighbor's report, the Grenil woman was on her knees washing clothes on the banks of the Laguna Fría when Second Police Inspector Félix Valenciano and Officer Norberto Ruiz, both dressed as civilians, shot her in the back. The police report stated:

> "At three p.m. in a site called Laguna Fría of this jurisdiction –Gan Gan Chubut- the death of Elena Greenhill occurred. The deceased was the widow of Coria. She was forty two years of age and of British nationality. She died as a result of two bullet wounds".

She had been shot in a lung and in the back of her head. Her lover, Martín Taborda, had also been wounded but managed to escape. Eventually, though, they caught up with him and he was arrested.

Félix Valenciano and his aide were accused of murder. He was in prison for a year and then, as so often happened in the case of brave policemen, he was set free. Some years later he murdered three shepherds but a stay of proceedings was declared for other crimes he had committed in return for some sinister "services rendered" to the police of different provinces. He ended his days as a rancher in Lago Argentino.

Elena Greenhill left her children a large amount of sheep she owned, a power of attorney to collect the money she was owed and the eleven thousand pesos that were destined to buy land (which they received much later) and that she was carrying when she was killed.

The Englishwoman was a calculating person who methodically planned all her actions. She was quite a passionate woman and most attractive. Men were fascinated by her appealing personality.

The only time she was careless was that time in Laguna Fría when she was shot in the back and killed. The English journalist Rose Forbes described her as:

> "An outlaw, known as "the Englishwoman", who always carried a gun in her blouse and a rifle under the saddle. She successfully murdered her first husband. Then, in her lover's company, she pointed her gun at the head of an old admirer of hers to get hold of the forty thousand pesos which was the cost of the wool that had just been sold. They killed her without giving her the opportunity to surrender".

A Texan sheriff

Nobody knows the exact date when the Texan Martin Sheffield came to Patagonian lands with the idea of settling down. Some references establish it at the end of the 80´s, others half way through the 90´s. There was, however, unanimous coincidence in that he was an imaginative story-teller, full of fun and always telling jokes.

Sheffield herded cattle whistling; he was an excellent shot and, as far as drinking was concerned, nobody could beat him.

He rode all the way through the Patagonian desert on his white mare. There was no farm, *rancho* or *boliche* where he wasn´t known. Besides, everybody knew –told by him, naturally- that he´d been a sheriff in Texas; he had a metal badge to prove it.

Apparently it was the gold rush that urged him to come to Patagonia. But then he took many different jobs: from gold prospector to drover, also hunter and scout-guide in several official missions.

He was an expert *truco* and *taba* player. And his marksmanship was a legend. Rumors had it that he caught trout shooting, and that he could easily shoot a cigarette from the lips of anybody who dared him; he also enjoyed shooting holes into the heels of women´s shoes.

PATAGONIA

But many inhabitants of Patagonia agreed that this man of the west would have been forgotten if it hadn´t been for the discovery of an antediluvian beast in the Epuyén lake. Apparently Sheffield was not the first to discover the monster; it was first seen by an employee of the firm Pérez Gabito, who gave the terrifying news to the ex-sheriff of Texas.

Maybe he shared his discovery with Sheffield because the latter had been a guide in several expeditions organized by paleontologists and naturalists, in fact one of these had resulted in the discovery of the fossil of a plesiosaurus. In any case, Sheffield was not only a person who had personal contacts with scientists...he was also a drinking partner...

On January 19th 1922 Sheffield wrote a letter to the director of the Zoological Gardens, Clemente Onelli. In it he relates having seen "in the middle of the lagoon, a monster with a head like an enormous swan", and that by the way the water moved he gathered the beast could have "a body similar to a crocodile". Onelli himself signed the first announcement of this discovery in the newspaper *"La Nación"*. Besides, *"La Prensa"* also stated that the "presence of specimens of unsuspected beings in Patagonia would bring great prestige to this region" (it did not specify what suspicion it referred to). And *Crítica*, a popular newspaper, headlined the article "The Dragon of Capadocia". *La Fronda* was most skeptical about all this, and mentioned that this "millenary, apocalyptic animal makes a hell of a noise and usually appears in the midst of vapors emanating from drunken *gringos"*.

Clemente Onelli loved Patagonia and admired all those who explored its territory, who investigated and pursued a physical and ethnical knowledge of this region. He sympathized with all those who fought towards an adequate demarcation of its boundaries. We could say that he felt Patagonia as a life concern and that, therefore, he was going to make the most of this unexpected stroke of luck brought about by the "monster" and the ensuing publicity. He even went to the extreme of suggesting the plesiosaurus could be embalmed...The Jockey Club took up the gauntlet and requested the exclusive rights to be the first to show it (we presume the request was presented to the Natural Sciences Museum).

In the meantime, the Society for the Prevention of Cruelty to Animals presented an outraged complaint against the circus-type treatment the beast was submitted to.

The news even echoed in the United States of America, although *The New*

York Times took a distant attitude and simply headlined "Ghosts in Patagonia". In Philadelphia there was an attempt to organize an expedition of geologists and paleontologists, while the Museum of Natural History of New York evaluated the possibility of sending a research committee.

A group of researchers left Buenos Aires loaded with syringes, reflectors, formol, torches, ropes and even…dynamite. Public subscriptions were promoted. A lady of the "porteño" high society who didn't want to make her name public donated one thousand five hundred pesos. Atlántida, the publishing firm, donated one thousand pesos, and there were other people of different social standing who made their personal contributions.

An emotional appeal to patriotic feelings was also displayed. Some North American scientists suggested the convenience (if and when the prehistoric beast was captured) of transferring it to the U.S.A. for a "more thorough investigation". This of course was staunchly opposed by *Diario del Plata,* who considered it "abided by the discriminatory principles of the Monroe Doctrine".

Two mentally deranged patients escaped from a mental institution determined to fight against the beast. They were caught before they were able to confront it.

In spite of all the noisy publicity given to this prehistoric monster, no actual proof of its existence ever appeared, and people's interest gradually dwindled away.

Some time later, Clemente Onelli urged all those who were interested in the fascinating Patagonian territory to

> *"practice some andean gym climbing its wild hills, and to enjoy its primitive, beautiful landscapes which are, unfortunately, too remote to foster in youths the strong, healthy passion for nature and mountain climbing".*

Sheffield had a half-breed son who inherited his father's passion for gin and the sheriff's metal star he always carried pinned to his breast-pocket. The mythical storyteller and inventor of fables was killed in 1936 by delirium tremens. He was buried next to the stream of Ñorquincó.

> *"This man of the west knew a lot of people, and what he didn't hear he guessed. He knew who abided by the law and who didn't. He had a lasting friendship with John Evans, whom he visited regularly in his house in Trevelin. Sheffield continued searching for*

gold even though it was practically exhausted. Whenever he found some low-gold nuggets he swapped them with Evans for flour. A great friend of the Welsh pioneer once said: "I think this was a respectful and charitable gesture on John's part".

15.- THE NEW HEROES

The brave Patagonian teachers - Juan Chayep, Vicente Calderón, Francisco Giglio, Isaías Vera, Raúl Díaz and other schoolmasters - The passion for teaching meant putting up with isolation, endless distances, unrelenting climate and unproductive land

They were teachers. They taught wherever they could, and whichever way possible. They usually started out in huts, which they soon turned into *ranchos*, and, much later, in primitive buildings with two or three classrooms. Sometimes they moved from one camp to another taking the school with them, sharing with the tribe their meager, makeshift existence, trying to stimulate children who were underfed, overridden with lice, filth and diseases.

First, the man slaughtered a sheep. Then he kneaded dough and baked some bread. After that he asked the children to follow him and they walked a long way until they got to a clay quarry. Between them they collected a large amount of clay and transported it to a *rancho* in a desolate site of Chubut called Cañadón Bagual. The low corrugated iron roofed *rancho* was their school. This man was the teacher Juan Chayep and the children, his pupils. All these kids' parents were illiterate (Chileans or local Indians), some of them lived several miles from the school and yet they never missed the classes given by this teacher they both loved and respected.

In summer the corrugated iron roof got so hot that the school resembled an oven. So, Chayep improvised an outdoor classroom and lessons were held under a sackcloth awning. The students were most attentive and, following their teacher's instructions, they learnt how to turn the clay into plates, glasses, pots and pans that they afterwards baked in rudimentary ovens they themselves built.

Chayep was the son of humble Arab immigrants. He was quite used to fighting arid lands and a life of hardships. Rather than shy away from difficulties, he faced them and tried to find his away about making the most of his resourcefulness. He used to get water from a small brook and, with the help of his pupils, turned an arid patch of land into a vegetable garden.

He was aware that hunger, extreme heat or cold and illiteracy were not the only enemies he had to contend with. There were also the boredom and monotony, enhanced by the melancholy of the unending gray tableland.

The pupils were always punctual and never missed their classes. It was their way of showing just how much they enjoyed and appreciated their teacher's resourcefulness and the effort he made to turn a class into an amusing and interesting experience.

In time, the parents and other local inhabitants also went to the *escuela-rancho*. Not as students, but as lookers-on.

Chayep had a cat that went along with him everywhere. Sometimes he used to talk to the cat. Of course, the only response he ever got was a Miauu!. But he thought it would be a good idea to try and "talk" with the cat using ventriloquism. He did so and became quite an expert. Then he added a few tricks of magic, and with time he developed a sort of show that he put on every time there was some feast day, to the delight of all the spectators who were most surprised at this "cat who talked with the teacher".

Another time, Chayep had been named teacher at a school right by the lake Futalaufquén. The premises were in a most ruinous condition, weeds invading every corner of the ramshackle building. Water leaked everywhere, the pupils sat on old boxes, everything was dirty and damp.

Chayep immediately requested funds and a loan to finance the necessary repairs. As he wasn't able to gather all the money that was needed he asked the owner of a sawmill to allow him to work on Sundays and feast days using the tools of his establishment. Permission granted, he then asked the pupils and the neighbors to collaborate, and all together they managed to weed the land and rebuild the school with wooden planks and tree trunks that he cut down and prepared at the sawmill.

When the house was finished, he surrounded it with a fence, a garden and an orchard. In the back yard he built a shed with a workshop. They worked as a community, and while the neighbors helped build the house, the teacher cooked lunch for them. Finally, the new school was inaugurated on the 25th of May 1929.

But he still had other plans in mind. Once the school was inaugurated he installed an aqueduct which carried water from a stream to the school bathroom, thus providing it with hot water. He also improvised a casing of stream-water in tubes and generated power which provided the school with electricity. That meant they were able to listen to the radio, and the pupils could use an electric lathe to carry out their practical works.

A fund-raising committee for the school destined a sum of money to feed the pupils, and Chayep (using his own money) immediately built a barn which became the school dining-room.

After tedious negotiations and plenty of red tape, Chayep finally managed to have a plot of land granted to the school where an adequate building was later built.

Vicente Calderón was another dedicated Patagonian teacher. He arrived in Cholila in October of 1905 after riding for a month and four days. His parting point was the Welsh colony in Gaimán, seven hundred and fifty kilometers away from his new destination.

The moment he arrived he started to build the hut that would later be used as a school. Using mud and wooden beams, after seven months' hard work he erected a humble but solid school which would officially replace the private school that had, up to that moment and for three years, functioned in the house of the colonist Sixto Gérez.

But there were other things that worried Calderón. He had found out that the Chilean firm Compañía Cochamó had in mind an expansionist project, which included buying a part of the territory granted to Argentina in the border demarcation with Chile, in the regions of Cholila, Epuyén and El Bolsón. The land in question belonged to the landowner Florencio Martínez de Hoz, who was finally forced to put off the sale due to pressure put upon him by Indalecio Gómez, who was Interior Minister. All this was thanks to the action brought about by teacher Vicente Calderón, who confided his concern to Governor Julio B. Lezana who, in turn, asked the Minister to stop the sales operation.

The firm Compañía Cochamó was aware that the teacher had been the leading figure in the campaign carried out to prevent the purchase of those lands. Also aware of that fact were a couple of policemen in Cholila, Sergeant Elviro Cejas and Officer Antonio Battilana, both loyal to the Chilean firm (incidentally, it was the same firm that purchased the lands of Cassidy and Sundance).

So one evening, just after ten p.m., both policemen paid a call on Calderón, who politely asked them in. They sat in the kitchen, close to the fire, and then one of them went to the courtyard. He placed the gun between two of the wall's wooden poles and shot Calderón. The bullet went straight behind his right ear and into the fire. Without a moments' hesitation, Calderón ran into his bedroom to grasp his gun but he dropped to the floor, covered in blood. The aggressors thought he was dead and tried dragging him to a nearby pool, but he was too heavy for them so they just left him lying on the ground and got away. Shortly after Calderón recovered consciousness and heard the desperate screams of his *peón*. The policemen stabbed the *peón* to death.

Calderón managed to drag himself along five endless kilometers, falling down half the time, or clutching on to some bushes; the fact was that he managed to reach the house of his friend Sixto Gérez (Butch Cassidy's neighbor) where he was attended on promptly. They cleaned his wound and were finally able to stop the hemorrhage.

The next morning, at dawn, Calderón went on horseback to Esquel. He was worried that the police, now aware that he hadn't died, would go looking for him at his friend's house. He remembered that "it was three o'clock in the morning and the road was covered in snow."

It was only after a seven-hour ride that he received the necessary medical attention.

A month and a half afterwards he had completely recovered from his wounds and went back to Cholila. But the school inspector considered his presence there was still risky so it was decided to give him a new destination in the Indian colony of Nahuel Pan, in the vicinity of Esquel.

Four years went by before he was able to return to Cholila, where he carried out his work as teacher for eight more years.

The two policemen were tried and sent to jail.

Teacher Elías Francisco Giglio was a very determined man who never hesitated and never went back on his decisions.

The conditions of his school couldn't have been worse. It was the school N° 53, placed right in the middle of the Andean range, practically on the Chilean border, in a location called Hua-Hum. It was enclosed in a plot of around fifty hectares of forest-covered land. The beautiful scenery was counteracted by extreme climatic conditions: the snow, the freezing cold and the powerful winds were constant, unrelenting companions.

It was impossible to teach agriculture and cattle-breeding because of the barren soil and the lack of water for irrigation.

But Giglio wasn't daunted, and he visited all the neighboring sawmills to see what he could get. They agreed to provide him with free wood and he himself, out of his own pocket bought the necessary tools, nails, clamps, screws, etc. He gathered the eldest pupils of the school and, all together, set about building an aqueduct. A few days of hard work were sufficient to finish a one-hundred-and fifty-meters-long aqueduct which would transport water to the irrigation ditches. That way, the students were able to have their own vegetable garden.

He found that animal excrements and the detritus of tree leaves were not sufficient to fertilize the land. So he practically mortgaged all his income in the purchase of twenty sheep which would produce more manure and make the land more fertile.

All the students took part in the farming activities: sowing, tending the sheep, looking after the hen-house, devising tools and equipment that the teacher couldn't always afford to buy.

Gradually the school became an experimental farm, where they selected the adequate species for that particular soil and climate. Finally, they became purveyors of seeds for the local settlers. And, with time, it became a center of production of fruit trees (pears, plums, different types of apples) and assorted vegetables.

The students ate off the farm produce. There were even enough cows to cover the necessary daily milk ration.

The school was at forty-five kilometers' distance from the nearest village, San Martín de los Andes. Due to the lack of public transportation to cross the lake Lácar by boat, the only way of reaching the town was riding on horseback through the thickets. This isolation worried Giglio, who wondered how they could cope in case of an emergency.

One day he was leafing through a magazine, as was his habit in order to keep up with the news, and suddenly came across the plan of a do-it-yourself boat. He got to work on it without a moments' delay.

Somehow, he managed to buy a motor and before one year was up (which was the time it took him to build the raft in his free time) he finished the craft and launched it on the lake, reaching San Martín de los Andes after sailing thirty-five kilometers.

Since then, the boat became indispensable for all purposes. It was not only used as school transport, it was also necessary to distribute the farm production, to help neighbors in the event of any emergency, to carry the sick, or the doctors, and for every pressing matter that arose in the village.

Isaías Vera and Raúl B. Díaz will always be remembered as two of the most famous "itinerant teachers" in Patagonia. In Próspero Alemandri's words (he was an expert in educational matters),

> *"they wandered all over this "damned land" and they walked across and knew every inch of these immense territories".*

How did these teachers get to the farthest regions?

Usually on horseback, or in a mule-drawn wagon. Or herding cattle. Sleeping out-of-doors on their saddle and trappings. Cutting furrows in the snow to allow the carts to advance, with temperatures of twenty or more degrees C below zero. Putting up with hunger, cold and thirst in order to reach the place where they had to build a school, knead mud, cut adobe blocks, pull down trees, cut wood, make doors and benches,...

We can do no more than just mention some of the heroic and valuable deeds undertaken by these Patagonian rural teachers, who made the most of the meager means at their disposal thanks to their creative imagination, resourcefulness, tenacity and resilience.

16.- ATTEMPTS TO MAKE THE "CIUDAD DE LOS CESARES" COME TRUE

Influenced by Francisco P. Moreno's enthusiastic ideas, Minister Ezequiel Ramos Mejía, with the help of the North American scientist-geologist Bayley Willis, attempted to carry out the most modern and transforming project ever devised, as yet, for promoting progress in Patagonia – Obstacles and drawbacks – Meager development

Ever since the times of the conquest, Patagonia favored all kinds of stories and legends which suggested that wealth and riches were available, ready to be grasped without effort, like some sort of magic gift that Providence had set in store for any willing adventurer.

Nevertheless, all those fortune-seekers who dared to explore its thorny, sterile plateaus in this quest had to face countless problems: hunger, thirst, battles with the white man or against the native Indians, the overpowering desert, the frustrated attempts to establish colonies or settlements, extreme climatic conditions, etc., which showed the tragic other side of the tantalizing myth that gave a meaning to their lives.

On the other hand, there were two men who wouldn't submit to nature's tyrannical rule, quite the contrary: they tried to use it in their favor, driving them towards outsized, totally ambitious projects.

One of these men was Ezequiel Ramos Mejía, who was Minister during the governments of Roca, Figueroa Alcorta and Sáenz Peña. The other man was Bailey Willis, the North American geologist who was a public official of the Department of Geological Research of the United States of America.

Bailey Willis was an assistant member of the International Scientific Congress that was carried out in Buenos Aires, in 1910. He was by then a prominent personality in scientific circles: engineer in Mining, PHD in Geology and Civil Engineering graduated from Columbia University, New York, and also very respected in Europe and in Asia.

Minister Ramos Mejía asked him to observe the drill for water that was taking place in the province of San Juan. He needed his opinion as a geologist. They afterwards had a private conversation in which Bailey Willis explained to the Minister that those works would end up in failure because of the inadequate geological conditions. The Minister was most upset but further investigation proved Bailey Willis was right: they had already drilled over five hundred meters and all in vain.

This episode allowed Ramos Mejía to evaluate Bailey Willis' expertise. He knew he was the man he needed for the plans he had in mind and promptly proposed that he take over the exploration of Patagonia in search of drinking water.

Bailey Willis was interested in Patagonia, it had a kind of mysterious quality which intrigued him, so he gladly accepted the offer. He agreed to carry out a preliminary topographic survey of the land, and then, in a second instance, the geological investigation of the territory between San Antonio and Nahuel Huapi. He traveled to the United States to assemble a team of specialists and the necessary equipment.

Emilio E. Frey, who had collaborated with the "Perito" Moreno, was appointed chief assistant of the project.

That marked the starting point of the Committee of Hydrological Studies of the Ministry of Public Works of Argentina.

Once the preliminaries were over, Bailey Willis traveled down south. Even though for him it was unexplored land, in many ways it resembled the Wild West of his own country, where natives were pursued and bandits and outlaws imposed their codes of violence throughout the territory.

It certainly had all the dangers and drawbacks of the North American Wild West. Unfortunately, it lacked some of its advantages, such as the tenacity shown by the hard-working settlers that were the core of its colonization.

This geologist had witnessed the process of population growth in the North American West; he knew that villages which had started off on a very primitive basis soon became important cities. He came from an active, practical country that wanted all the programmed studies to be carried out because there were industries anxiously waiting, and professionals and workmen and everything that was involved in the creation of a new location.

Therefore, he couldn't understand why bureaucracy had delayed the expedition, formed by four young and experienced North American topographers and geologists, two Argentine engineers and Frey and Bailey Willis himself. They also took with them two expert scouts, eighty mules and forty horses. They were delayed for two whole weeks on account of the red tape involved. Finally, Minister Ezequiel Ramos Mejía had to intervene personally to get things done.

All this was beyond Bailey Wills's comprehension: "I just can't understand why all this happens in a country where things must be done from scratch...!

Six months looking for water in Valcheta, and still no water appeared... Before giving up the project, Willis decided to carry out a careful examination of the place where the stream originated. He built dams to store the water surging from the springs under an extension of lava, and also a canal which would divert the water course to the port of San Antonio. That way, the needs of the people of San Antonio could be met and four thousand hectares could receive adequate irrigation.

The Committee warned Minister Ramos Mejía that irrigation would increase the value of these fiscal lands considerably. Besides, irrigation could rescue the arid lands of northern Patagonia and make them apt for farming purposes.

Minister Ramos Mejía was very pleased about these reports, but his enthusiasm was not shared by certain circles of Congress and the Government.

The Committee of Hydrological Studies had been granted one hundred thousand pesos. Willis was a very strict administrator and kept all the invoices and receipts that accounted for all their expenses. So, by the time the Committee had spent eighty-one thousand pesos, he duly presented all necessary papers and asked for a reimbursement. Nevertheless, in Buenos Aires, not only did they not send him the money, they also invented ridiculous excuses for not doing so. For example, they once rejected an invoice, and by doing so blocked its payment, because five cents were missing.

"As one cannot send money by mail I sent a five cent stamp -explained Willis to Ramos Mejía- but they returned it saying that the payment had to be in cash. So I wrote back asking if I could send a personal check."

Ramos Mejía was with the "Perito" Moreno when Willis was telling him about all these silly obstacles posed by members of the government. The Minister was seething with rage.

Moreno had been the inspired promoter of his plans and a great admirer of

Willis and his works.

In an article Arturo Frondizi wrote on "Bailey Willis and the second conquest of the desert", he alluded to the typical train of thought during those times, to "the typical mentality of the Centennial society, unable to think of any economic problem other than good crops and meat for export".

Finally, in October of 1911 Willis presented his survey to the Minister, complete and finished, guaranteeing the provision of water to San Antonio for a population of ten thousand inhabitants, the rural areas and cattle grazing within the twenty-four-kilometer-wide area at either side of the railroad alongside a hundred kilometer stretch.

The Board of Irrigation, which was against investments in Patagonia, together with the legislators who criticized it, managed to block the project.

In Bailey Willis's notes he remarked that:

> "The attacks in Congress on Minister Ramos Mejía and his whole policy towards national development continued relentlessly".

Six months after the formal presentation of Willis's survey Julián Romero, chairman of the Board of Irrigation, informed that the report had been taken to his private home in order to give it careful consideration but that

> "unfortunately his house had been burnt down and so had the report".

Luckily, Bailey Willis was not only a clever man, he had also learnt by that time that he must be on his guard, and had taken the necessary precautions: the report he presented was a copy of the original which he kept safely, under lock and key, in Valcheta.

Neither Ramos Mejía nor Bailey Willis, who counted with Francisco Moreno's firm support, were to be daunted by this bureaucratic sabotage. The North American geologist always compared the Minister's projects with the ventures of several industrial firms in the Far West which he had formed part of, that had achieved their objective of establishing large population centers, industries, farming concerns and mining firms together with a vast network of public services and communications.

They were already considering the possibility of building a railway from San Antonio to the Pacific passing through Nahuel Huapi, to promote economic growth both in Argentina and in Chile. Bailey Willis, who was amazed at the natural resources and possibilities of the region, was absolutely sure that the vast zone that was being explored could have a future as promising as that of the Far West in his own country.

In carrying out the surveys to build this railway he found similar drawbacks to those they had to face in the U.S.A.

Of course, it was possible to avoid building expensive railway bridges and replacing them with wooden bridges calculated to last for twenty five years. By that time, both population and production would have increased considerably and they would be able to afford masonry bridges because the cost would be entirely justified.

Ramos Mejía viewed the railway to Valdivia as part of a colossal project which was based on the creation of industries, hydro-electrical stations, dams and roads, farming and cattle-breeding establishments, irrigation and the settlement of large communities.

The contrast between the changes these visionary men dreamed of and what was actually being carried out in Patagonia escapes all comprehension. Their plans had in mind a present projected towards the future. Instead, real life in the south showed a clinging to the past.

In those days, sheep breeding was a regular activity in Patagonia. Not much manpower was required, usually it meant hiring a few Chilean *peones* who crossed the border when it was time for sheep shearing. The establishments most apt for rearing sheep were the large *estancias*. The larger the better, because wool was only profitable if it was sold in large quantities.

The 1895 census registered 500 inhabitants in Río Gallegos, who were mainly distributed in *estancias*. 150 inhabitants in Santa Cruz, 60 in San Julián and 50 in Deseado. Europeans totaled 750 inhabitants while the native Argentines just barely reached 15.

At that time there was an intensive hunting for the local fauna because any harm to the herds of sheep had to be avoided, no matter what the cost. Buenos Aires was an avid consumer of *quillangos*, ostrich feathers and furs of different animals, all doomed to extinction.

The natives were also considered from a cost-and-profit angle. The only profit was to prevent them from eating sheep. Worse still, Indians had a price: one pound sterling for "every ear or genital organ". In the end only the genitals were demanded and paid for because that ensured the native's death; otherwise, if only the ears were cut off, there was danger of the hunter going soft, collecting his pay and letting the Indian go (minus an ear, but alive). Sometimes, whenever one of the landowners had a whim, he ordered the burning of all the Indians' *ranchos*, and had the natives and their families driven out.

On the other hand, the States' policy for the distribution of land benefited a small minority of large landowners, in shameless disregard of the advice given by Sarmiento, Moreno and Moyano to establish colonies and increase the population.

According to the statistics calculated by Horacio Lafuente (Santa Cruz, 1920/1921), around 20 million hectares were distributed among 619 *estancias*, but one sole person or company could own or have shares in several other *estancias*, or else use figureheads. These statistics show that these large extensions of land belonged to 189 Argentines, 110 Spaniards, 81 English, 53 Chileans, 42 French and 37 Germans.

The territory was a man's land. The above mentioned census counted 748 men and 310 women. Nearly twenty years later, over a total of 9948 inhabitants, there were 7111 men and 2837 women.

The "Perito" Moreno sadly compared the abandonment of the Patagonian territory with the colonization policy of the United States. He considered the U.S.A. was "on the way to becoming the first country in the world because of the knowledge its children have of their national soil and the resources work provides".

In September of 1911 the Chamber of Deputies summoned Minister Ramos Mejía who was accused of "squandering public money" in the case of the Committee of Hydrographic Studies. He was ordered to resign, but President Sáenz Peña asked him to remain in his post.

Regardless of all this legal battle, Bailey Willis continued his research for the Ramos Mejía project. Exploration of the area between Junín de los Andes and the south of Nahuel Huapi led him to conclude that, due to its natural resources, climate and soil, it was possible to promote the settlement of three million inhabitants.

It had everything: adequate soil for farming and cattle-breeding, enough forests to feed an important wood industry and hydraulic energy.

Bailey Willis was of the opinion that the Argentine Republic could eventually become independent of foreign manufactures. The southern region had to attract population on a permanent basis and create the industries necessary for the transformation of its raw material.

Emilio Frey was a member of the Committee and had a profound knowledge of the south. Together with Bailey Willis they began to study the possibilities of all the local trees. They discovered *coihue* wood could produce excellent pulp to make paper. Just to make sure they sent samples to be analyzed in the laboratory specializing in wood products in the U.S.A., which confirmed their idea was correct.

Ramos Mejía confided to Bailey Willis that part of his project included founding a capital city which would be the headquarters of the provincial government, with its university (16 hectares were set apart for the Industrial and the Arts University) military barracks, industrial and residential districts. He commissioned Willis to find the right location and draw up the plans.

The Committee devoted its full attention to working on the project that would later figure in the report "North of Patagonia". Figures revealed that, over an overall sum of 76 million pounds worth of imported goods, 15 million were spent on fabrics, wood and its manufactures, paper, leather goods, etc. Bailey Wills considered that, in the near future,

> *"the hydroelectric force of the river Limay will be used for the production of wool fabrics and jersey with the soft fleece of merinos of Río Negro and Neuquén; other woolen goods will be produced using the coarse material of Chubut and Santa Cruz. Leather goods with the production of the meat packing houses, furniture and other wood products, and even chemical substances from the beech tree woods. Also, nitrates to be used as fertilizers".*

Willis's project evaluated the Patagonian hydroelectric potential in around 6.824.000 metric HP, and he couldn't help comparing it with those of the Niagara Falls (5.800.000).

There were so many things Willis failed to understand....

He often wondered why, considering the huge wool production in Patagonia, it wasn't washed and processed on the spot. That meant it was sent, dirty and in bulk, to be industrialized somewhere else! Of course, there were powerful interests opposed to any measures which promoted growth and development: the owners of large Patagonian estates, the exporters and some government officials who could profit from them and who were also involved with British interests. Great Britain provided its industries with the non-processed wool it imported from Argentina and wanted to keep things that way. If Argentina started to industrialize its own wool, the British would be the first to suffer.

As usually happens, there is always a voice that sings out of tune. As Frondizi said in his essay, referring to "an archaic military-strategic concept" which

> "...made sure that these regions remain uninhabited and in a state of abandonment to avoid possible invasions (this theory was considered "rancid" by an army strategist. And the air force has put it away in some forgotten files, because, to my humble way of thinking, the best defense is brought about by material progress)".

Both the project promoted by the Committee Bailey Willis presided and Minister Ramos Mejía's intention of erecting the Industrial City of Nahuel Huapi faced the strong opposition of wool exporters, importers of fabrics and the British railway companies, whose directors were alarmed at the prospect of having to compete with state-managed railroads. Ramos Mejía was also interested in importing Chilean raw materials to have them industrialized in Patagonia.

Congress denied the necessary funds to prepare the project and carry it out. Bailey Willis cleverly suggested that "Ramos Mejía represented the intelligent governing class, and the politicians that opposed him, elected by non-intelligent masses, were at the service of the Invisible Empire of capital which held both under its strict control".

During a conversation with the General Manager of the "Ferrocarril del Sud", the latter confessed to Bailey Willis that

> "the creation of national railroads is not suitable to the interests of the Ferrocarril del Sud, because it means having a future competitor in Patagonia".

In the end, Ramos Mejía was forced to resign; Sáenz Peña was at that moment a very sick man so he was replaced by Victorino de la Plaza who, in turn, appointed Manuel Moyano as his new Minister. Moyano did everything in his power to destroy the project; he accused Bailey Willis of embezzlement and threatened to send him to jail. The basis of his accusation was that the money had been sent and there were still no signs of the report. But a few days later, a very disappointed Minister held in his hands the first volume of "Northern Patagonia".

When Moyano saw his plan had failed he set his mind on stopping the second volume from being published. He was really following orders from the British Railways company, of which he had once been a Director.

The "Perito" Moreno and Bailey Willis vainly tried to distribute the first volume of the report. And as for the second volume, it was never published. The survey contained very modern projects. Apart from the railway connecting San Antonio-San Martín-Valdivia it also outlined a road network and the use of steamboats in lakes.

The North American geologist also predicted important developments in the meat and dairy products industries, and of farming activities in general.

In view of the significant industrial population that would settle in that region (which was destined to become the main center of Argentine production), Bailey Willis considered that Patagonia was only half a century behind his country's West.

On the other hand, a national Senator was of the opinion that
"the only thing Patagonia needs is an efficient Justice Department and plenty of policemen".

The North American geologist was full of praise for Emilio Frey, doctor Moreno's right-hand man. "Don Emilio" alone discovered more than seventy lakes.

He finished his elementary school in Baradero and his parents then sent him to Switzerland for high school and university studies. Once he graduated he returned to Argentina; he was the first Engineer in Topography in the country.

Emilio Frey then began to work in the Museum of La Plata under Francisco P. Moreno's direction. He later carried out significant research in Patagonia. During his explorations he suffered all kinds of hardships and went through situations of extreme danger. In the river Kruger there is a notice saying "In this place the engineer Emilio E. Frey was shipwrecked in April 1898". That happened when he was returning from the border pass Navarro and, after exploring the lakes Stange and Kruger, decided to sail along the river Futaleufú. That river was unknown at that moment, and the rapids took him by surprise. So powerful were the waves crashing against the rocks that the boat capsized. He himself was wrenched away from the sinking boat and left churning in a whirlwind of enraged waters, abandoned to his own resources. He didn't know how he managed to overcome that situation. He guessed it was Providence, that he was destined to finish his voyage safely. The fact was that he didn't know how he survived, in a way it was like a miracle.

He concluded that Futaleufú was no river, it was more like a hell-born blast of wind churning up enormous waves that crashed between granite walls.

The three *chilotes* (Chileans from Chiloé island) accompanying him, "fearless men and expert sailors", all died.

That was the first attempt to navigate that river and its tragic end.

Frey was really very upset about losing these men whom he valued and respected. He decided to continue his exploration on foot. But he fared no better:

> *"We had already been three days without food and five fighting against the elements.*
> *Walking through the bush we were overridden by hunger and fatigue. Our clothes reduced to rags and the soles of our boots worn out. Half naked and staggering, we managed to go on our way guided, I guess, by the instinct of survival and the strong desire to reach our goal.*
> *Everybody was exhausted.*
> *-"Master, I can go no further, I stay here..." –and two of my good, faithful chilotes just lay down on the ground".*

They finally reached camp. The men were half asleep and dropped to the ground and Frey got them to sip some *caña*. Much later, and still semi-unconscious, they were able to eat a light meal, the first bite in five days.

Afterwards, they smeared grease all over their bodies to remove the thorns that had stuck in the skin. There were small thorns (like those of the *calafate*)and even splinters from the *coihue* and cypress trees.

Between 1893 and 1903, Frey was at the head of an exploring committee, under "perito" Moreno's direction. They were hard years of rough living.

Later, he also formed part of the committee that dealt with the border conflict with Chile.

Many years later, after so many decades of exploring in extremely demanding situations, he naïvely remarked to a high ranking official of Parques Nacionales: "Even though you may find it hard to believe, I also was young once". In a way, he was insinuating that he had to face the responsibilities of a grown man when he was still a young boy .

The official, who was no other than Diego Neill, promptly answered:

> *"It's hard to determine. Because from the point of view of your*

spirit, health, mind and sense of humor, you're just as young nowadays".

None of these talented scientists, militant and visionary men, lived to see their dreams of a prosperous Patagonia come true. Ramos Mejía, Francisco P. Moreno, Emilio Frey and their great friend Bailey Willis believed in a project and its feasibility.

What went wrong?

When approached for a personal opinion, an investigator ironically posed a question:

"Could it be geographic destiny?" He mused *"There's North America, let's say the United States. In the Civil War, the North won. And then there's South America, let's say Argentina. Here, it's the South that won".*

17.- LOOKING BACK

"I have the feeling that Patagonia is the most desolate of places... a land of exile, a place of de-territoriality" (Jean Baudrillard)

At the beginning of 1994, the *New York Times* sent Nathaniel C. Nash to inquire and write about Patagonia. In his report he singled out sheep breeding among other activities, and went on to explain that it was carried out in *estancias* which were established during the last century, and that helped Argentina become one of the richest countries in the world.

Some time later, the French thinker Jean Baudrillard wrote:

> "Behind the fantasy of Patagonia lies the myth of disappearance, of drowning in the desolation of the end of the world. Of course, this is just a metaphor. I can imagine that traveling to Patagonia is like reaching the limit of a concept, like getting to the end of things. I know Australia and the North American desert, but I have the feeling that Patagonia is the most desolate of places [...] a land of exile, a place of de-territoriality".

Even though Nathaniel C. Nash's impression lacked the philosophical scope of the French thinker, it did in a way predict a probable extinction when he announced that in Patagonia (a place of legends and adventures, which was once inhabited by *gauchos*, visited by Charles Darwin and a place where Cassidy and Sundance Kid roamed about), the land and the means of subsistence of its people were gradually disappearing. Patagonia was colonized in the XIX Century by people who came from Wales, Scotland and South Africa, and it prospered thanks to the breeding of sheep; these settlers gathered in closely knit ethnical groups and nowadays are witnesses to the disappearance of their legacy and traditions. For example the Afrikaans and the Old Welsh are languages that once prevailed throughout vast extensions of Patagonia and are nowadays hardly ever spoken.

The first sheep raisers came from the Malvinas islands, attracted by the promotion that Carlos María Moyano carried out in order to encourage settlements in Santa Cruz. The promotion consisted in granting facilities to those who wanted to own land. Since the latter years of XIX Century until the beginning of the XX Century, they gradually settled in the outskirts of Río Gallegos, San Julián, Santa Cruz and Lago Argentino. They worked very hard putting up with all kinds of extreme situations, the never ending desert, the loneliness, arid lands, cruel winds...Many of them grew old and, in a state of ill health, retired to Buenos Aires or Great Britain. Others, like William Halliday, who traveled to Scotland in 1908 with the idea of settling down in the place where he was born, finally felt homesick and returned to Patagonia to stay for good.

These men had to fight every day of their lives with situations that were dramatic because of the extreme conditions imposed on them by the environment. Herding the flocks could take months, and during that time they put up with lack of food, the bitter cold, the icy wind, even the attack from some *puma* or the onslaught of cattle thieves.

There was one famous drove of sheep which lasted more than two years, leaving Buenos Aires, going through Río Negro and ending in Santa Cruz. The shepherds were John Hamilton, Tomás Saunders, G. Mac Clain and Enrique Jamieson. During their journey they shared many evenings by the fire with important personalities, government officials, Francisco P. Moreno and many other explorers.

They advanced slowly, crossing mountains, wading across rivers, sometimes stopping and setting up camp when it was time to shear, or to wait for the lambs to be born. But always on the alert, guns at hand lest they suffered some sort of attack. Sometimes they got lost...and it took them some time to find the right way again.

Carlos Burmeister was a scientist and explorer who had been appointed to lead a mission for the National Museum and happened to meet the Scottish sheep-men on the banks of the river Chico. They sat around the fire and chatted until dawn and then parted company. A few days later, the Museum expedition set up camp some leagues further and after wading across the river Chico, they suddenly saw signs of a fire ahead. Burmeister gave the order to answer what he interpreted as a signal and shortly after a rider came galloping towards them: it was Saunders.

They had got into high plateaus and steep ravines when the Scotsmen soon realized the guide was heading towards the West. They had lost the way to San Julián. Saunders was left in charge of finding the right track, so he got hold of the two best horses and started riding towards the South East. He galloped three days running and had made his first stop the night before, one kilometer away from the National Museum camp. By observing the horseshoe prints on the damp soil he was able to follow their trail. So, certain they would see him, he climbed onto a plateau and lit a fire,.

Burmeister asked him to join them; then they would go to a pond nearby and from there he would show him the exact direction to San Julián.

In those days it was quite common for a shepherd to lose his way, it was just one of the many obstacles he had to face. Nevertheless, all these hardworking men had made their fortune. Contrary to the harsh, merciless experiences they had to deal with in their work, their private lives evolved in the shelter of a tightly woven community.

Rose Forbes, the English journalist who visited Patagonia, wrote down her acute impressions in several chronicles. She quoted a Scottish cattle-breeder's opinions:

> "I must admit I prefer sheep rather than people. Sheep don't make mistakes and they must surely have some sort of intelligence because they do have a memory. Once they've fallen into some place it is very difficult to oblige them to go to that same place, even after an interval of several months".

Forbes reflected:

> "Patagonia, this land in the uttermost part of the world, belongs to the sheep. Its aristocracy is represented by the Australian "merinos" [...] One half of Patagonia lives off the rearing of sheep, the other half, by stealing them".

The production of sheep became very important because it was directly stimulated by the textile industries in Europe. But nothing evolved around it, not even rudimentary agricultural activity, nor wool washing industries, nor any kind of manufacture, much less local colonies. With the few Chilean *peones* that crossed the border it was quite enough.

Apart from the Scotsmen, there were quite a number of German, French and Spanish sheep breeders who owned vast extensions of land.

During the First World War sales decreased. Wool prices went down, and besides there were new competitors such as Australia and New Zealand, all of which had a negative influence on the income of Patagonian wool merchants.

Worried about the situation, the Government in 1908 tried to stimulate population growth by granting facilities to families who would be willing to settle down and start some small farming concern in the area. But no change was brought about.

Imbalance turned the place into a man's land, the number of men outweighing that of women by a long stretch.

The wool crisis caused a breakdown of the local economy, which of course had its repercussion in the urban centers, and most of all it affected the staff working on *estancias*.

Social unrest became manifest in a few protesting groups. Workers' strife was more intense in Santa Cruz, and in 1921 the intervention of an army regiment commanded by Coronel Varela created a full-range commotion throughout the country: Varela gave the order to shoot down hundreds of *peones* who were on strike, having previously dug their own collective graves.

This massive killing gave rise to vehement debates in the Congress of Buenos Aires, in the midst of generalized indignation. Spokesmen of Hipólito Yrigoyen's government alleged that the only purpose of repressing the riot organized by anarchists was to prevent the plunder and burning of the premises and/or the seizure of hostages. The newspaper *Magellan Times* referred only to a "gang of rebels" of which "only those villains who gave a bad example had been executed".

On the other hand, those representing the Socialist Party denounced that the exploitation typical of the vast extensions of land promoted no alternative for the territory's development.

Settlements would make no difference demographically speaking, furthermore, they would just increase pauperization and encourage abusive labor conditions for the *peones*.

The Boers, descendants from the Dutch that settled in South Africa since 1652, had just been defeated by the British in 1899. Many Boers decided to emigrate and a group arrived in Patagonia. In 1902 they were given seventy leagues of land north of Comodoro Rivadavia. The soil was quite different to that of the Transvaal, which in a way explains why a new settler envisaging his Patagonian future, exclaimed: Oh, my God! What have I done to deserve this?

The lands of the Boer colony were no better than those of the valley of Chubut. On the other hand, this community of South African origin had farming experience and therefore had the necessary know-how. Being favored by springs which afforded them irrigation, they began planting vegetables. They surrounded their ranches with hedges and, when the farms were properly organized and producing goods, they started on sheep raising. They were efficient and persevering.

Three years after settling down they started manufacturing cheese which they sold in Comodoro Rivadavia, in addition to poultry and eggs.

Gorráiz Beloqui commented:

"It was a pleasure to approach their houses and behold their neat orchards decorating the ravines".

Some of the Boers chose to stay in town. One of them, a Mr. M.M. Venter, was the founder of an important store.

In 1905 a national decree increased the extension of the colony from 150.000 to 300.000 hectares. This, of course, helped to increase the development of the area, but, on the other hand, it also favored speculation in the sale of land. Indeed, some settlers who had paid one peso per hectare sold it at twenty and used the money to return to the country they originally came from.

A high official of the Ministry of Agriculture denounced agreements between the seller and the buyer; the latter was usually a rancher interested in enlarging his estate.

By law, it was obligatory to make improvements in the land before obtaining the right to ownership of the plot granted to the colonist. In spite of that, these improvements were not those required in a farm but what was demanded by the future buyer.

The first thirty Boer families finally got another settlement going. But the truth is that, except for the Welsh, colonists of other nationalities never managed to settle in large communities. Quite the contrary, as time went by, the Patagonian settlements resembled islets lost within a vast arid space of nearly 800.000 square kilometers, where only the Alto Valle del Rio Negro could capture important populations, with a fruit production that catered to the international markets.

Everything was on a small scale. Such was the case, for example, of the colony established by don Antonio Onetto (by appointment of the national Government) in 1884, in Puerto Deseado, with four European families (18 people). They suffered all kinds of hardships, including the death of Onetto two years after his arrival. Finally, the authorities left them abandoned to their luck.

All Carlos M. Moyano's attempts to attract colonists were frustrated on account of the way land was granted, because it only favored the breeding of sheep in large areas. And as only men were needed for that activity, it finally turned out that in some settlements there were 569.5 men for 100 women, while the percentage in the rest of the country was 115.5.

An economic survey carried out by the Centro Editor de America Latina stated that:

> "Colonization, considered as a systematic extraction of regional resources, brought about an exceedingly localized population: estancias and stations, mining camps, etc. The number of inhabitants was limited to what was strictly necessary for each activity. Men on their own, whose only company was often that of dogs and sheep, settled down in stations far from the manor house which was the only place suitable for human contact. That's where the wives and children of the owners or the managers or administrators of the establishment lived together.
>
> This social and economic disjointedness (during the decade of the 50's) expresses itself, among other things, in a high rate of suicides. Santa Cruz has a potential rate of 32 suicides per annum over a population of 84.500 inhabitants, which brings us to a rate of 37 in 100.000 inhabitants, which is higher than that of West Berlin (35 for every 100.000}, one of the highest in the world".

The pioneer Andreas Madsen, in certain parts of his "Old Patagonia", gives a very accurate description of this adverse reality:

> "In vain I tried to convince Fred to remain where he was, in the best pastures of Viedma. "They're arriving with sheep -he used to answer- these fellow countrymen, and they'll be here any moment; and this chap Piaget, who came the same day as you did, he's looking around to buy some land for a company.

PATAGONIA

This place will be full of these damned woollies in no time (for some reason Fred loathed sheep), and if a company settles down we'll be banished, just like it always happened. If they were a small group of settlers it's no problem; there'd be rows and fighting but there'd be plenty of space for all of us; but if it's a company it will gobble everything up. You'll see".

We reached a place which Fred has christened "The last retreat". That name didn't stop them from turning us out, a couple of years later, together with all the small settlers of Viedma. I was the only one who stubbornly decided to resist, so I just retreated a few paces, right at the foot of the Fitz Roy, where I carried on fighting, my back to the wall".

Madsen was on his own. At that time he was 22 years of age.: "I remembered the words of a Hymn "Closer to you, my Lord", and that gave me the strength to remain on, to put up with what was to come".

He started to build his cabin and was so absorbed with his work that for two months he didn't realize he was alone. He was experimenting the satisfaction of the true pioneer, which comes from conquering and producing without predating.

"Destruction -he sustained- begins with the large companies and their heartless capital. What a pity the Government didn't decree some forty years back the reserve of twenty or thirty leagues for a national park in this beautiful place!"

Andreas Madsen also regretted the disappearance of thousands of deer, gray foxes and other kinds of species, which followed the rider without fear, and played around with the horses' legs or sat in a circle next to the fire, waiting for a piece of meat or a bone.

"I look at the forest as it is today, burnt down and bare, not a deer to be seen in miles" and the red fox that has become extinct..."

What most enraged Madsen was that the company, not content with cutting down what it wanted, burnt down and destroyed all the rest, killing deer just for the pleasure of killing, to see if the guns were in good shape, leaving the dead bodies to rot, just for fun...

Madsen presented the government with a request for a reserve of land to preserve the deer and the foxes and the woods.

We can consider his wish was granted many years afterwards, because it´s a fact that nowadays there is a definite concern about ecological and conservationist matters. At present, the inhabitant of Patagonia is conscious of the natural heritage under his care, and makes positive efforts towards avoiding the extinction of endangered species, and protecting the indigenous vegetation and forest lands.

The country of those who choose their own exile

August of 1991: the biting Patagonian wind scattered volcanic ashes all over Santa Cruz. They came from the Chilean Andes. The Hudson volcano had erupted.

Millions of hectares were buried under a thick layer of grayish powder, and more than a million sheep died under the ashes.

Jack Mac Lean, one of the descendants of the prosperous Scottish pioneers of the beginnings of the XX Century, resignedly accepted his loss. In no time his twenty thousand hectares became worthless. Four years after that disaster he still saw the ashes covering the dry grass the sheep ate while grinding their teeth. And sheep with no teeth couldn't survive.

Finally, nature prevailed over the strikes and the tragic events of 1921. Those establishments which once were big and powerful are now slowly dying because of the desertification of the soil, the devaluation of wool prices, and, finally, as a result of having introduced into those lands an exotic animal -the sheep- in such large quantities that it destroyed the fragile ecological balance.

The massive entry of those animals right after the conquest of the desert, an excess of pasturing and the consumption of bushes to use as fuel to fight the cold, the strong winds and scant rains, all these aspects led to an erosive process that has no return trip.

When the vegetation ran out the sheep stock diminished. That was nature's response to the irrational ways of land exploitation.

Ecologists are worried about the environmental problems: oil spills resulting in the death of thousands of penguins, indiscriminate fishing, forests without adequate protection against fires, etc.

The agronomists of INTA (Instituto Nacional de Tecnología Agropecuaria) are working with ecologists of the GTZ Agency of Germany as a team, trying to revert the present situation of the greater part of the Patagonian territory with barely one inhabitant per square kilometer.

Nathaniel C. Nash, newspaper correspondent of *The New York Times*, spoke to some of the descendants of those successful Scottish pioneers of the beginning of the century. They no longer had a flourishing economy like in the olden days, when the children were sent to study in English schools or as boarders to St. George´s School in Buenos Aires.

Nash was of the opinion that

"situations of poverty and need produce social changes".

That explains why many former sheep-breeders have turned their establishments into places that can attract tourists. John Gough, a sheep-breeder from Esquel, doesn´t beat around the bush. He frankly admitted to Nash: "Our only hope is to get some tourists".

At present, the main resources of the region are oil, gas, fishing and tourism.

Population is still scarce in this vast land. Settlements are few and far between, generally people gather in tight communities, in small urban centers that are scattered here and there along the desert. Every now and then there is an arrival of new inhabitants, many of which have a very idealized picture of life in Patagonia and very little in the way of projects or specific plans. These are apt to be soon disappointed.

What would have happened if Ramos Mejía´s project, shared by Bailey Willis, Francisco P. Moreno and other visionary men had been carried out? Would it have set a vigorous process of growth and social changes in motion?

That imaginative and ambitious project was annulled by reactionary forces embodied in the people who were exponents of a rural country in a period of transition; small people whose short-range vision led them to think they had succeeded.

Almost five hundred years have elapsed since the fearless times of the conquest; centuries marked by the heroism of the settlers, the illusions of many dreamers, the silent, persevering effort of scientists and explorers.

And yet, the inhabitant of Patagonia doesn´t dwell on memories of the past. His existence is nourished by a persistent, dramatic hope of future fulfillment.

EPILOGUE

Time goes by, centuries follow one another along the road of history, and it´s always the same magic: Patagonia has an aura of its own that has always excited the imagination of travelers of all times and from all over the world. Made of tales and legends, always luring the visitor into an imaginary world of possibilities, tempting him to act the leading part in his own adventure, proposing new visions, new dreams, new promises.

One can´t help remembering Darwin´s impression of this strange, vast territory:

> "...it takes possession of my mind (and it´s not only my case") "It must be because it opens a whole new horizon to one´s imagination".

Nowadays the visitor not only can admire the landscape visually, he can also explore it and feel it by practicing all kinds of sports: mountaineering, trekking, skiing, canoeing in wild, spectacular rivers, horse-riding, sea diving, fishing (trout and salmon), watching the arrival of the right whales, visiting the penguin colonies, sailing along the canals of Tierra del Fuego to Antarctica, walking through blazing hot deserts, exploring the glaciers, practicing ecological, archaeological or paleontology tourism, rural tourism, visiting hot springs or the beaches that lie at the foot of the cliffs, with caves and petrified forests.

Some of the patagonian landscapes have been declared by UNESCO "heritage of mankind"; just to mention a few, there is Península Valdez, the Perito Moreno glacier, the 7.300 year old cave paintings in the "Cueva de las Manos" of Río Pintura. In short, all the vast circuit that goes from the Atlantic to the Pacific ocean.

Population is scant in this large territory equivalent to a third of the area of Argentina. There are even sites which are completely uninhabited. Under-population is one of Patagonia´s main characteristics.

All along the Andean mountain range there are lakes, pools and rivers of remarkable beauty. Not to mention the forests and peaks whose powerful magnetism lures the most renowned mountain climbers to dare the heights of Fitz Roy, the Torre and the rock needles surrounding them.

Between the Cordillera de los Andes and the sea lie the steppes, an extension of desert that continues right through to the Atlantic. There the landscape changes into a succession of beaches, caves and cliffs, isthmus and bays where a large variety of birds and aquatic animals can be admired, ending in Ushuaia, Tierra del Fuego. This city, the last of the extreme South, has become a major attraction for tourists who come from all over the world to enjoy the unspoilt beauty of the "natural gateway" to the white continent, Antarctica.

There are many ways of getting acquainted with Patagonia: some prefer the peaceful contemplation of its varied landscapes aboard a modern cruiser or overland in comfortable vehicles. Others choose to re-enact past times, feel the excitement of discovery and conquest in pursuing the "adventure of Patagonia", where facing and overcoming the obstacles is a sport, and definitely part of the fun.

International celebrities come as simple tourists to ski or practice their favorite sport, and some of them end up buying ranches, or enough land to pursue their own projects, such as the Benettons, who started their own wool industry to use in their textile production.

European and North American businessmen have invested fortunes in buying land for the exploitation of tourism, fishing and even game parks for big game hunting (deer, wild boar, etc.).

After many years of visiting Patagonia, an important man in certain business circles was asked what it was that held such a powerful attraction over him. His answer was: "I can feel nature breathing…".

REFERENCES

Abeijón, Asencio, *Memorias de un carrero patagónico* (Galerna)
Almada, H. M., *Hechos y personajes de la Patagonia* (Continente)
Alvarez, José (Fray Mocho), *En el mar austral* (Eudeba)
Arciniega, Rosa, *Pedro Sarmiento de Gamboa* (Sudamericana)
Azara, Félix de, *Viajes por la América meridional* (Espasa Calpe)
Barros, Alvaro, *Indios, Fronteras y seguridad interior* (Hachette)
Biedma, José Juan, *Crónica histórica del Nahuel Huapi* (Emecé)
Borrero, José María, *La Patagonia trágica* (Americana)
Braun Menéndez, Armando, *Pequeña historia patagónica. Pequeña Historia fueguina. Pequeña historia magallánica. Pequeña Historia austral* (Editorial Francisco de Aguirre)
Bridges, E. Lucas, *El último confín de la tierra* (Marymar)
Caillet Bois, Teodoro, *"Viajes de exploración en la Patagonia", "Piedra Buena, su acción patriótica","La primera población de Chubut", "El mayor Mateo Gebhard"* (Argentina Austral)
Chatwin, Bruce, *En la Patagonia* (Sudamericana)
Darwin, Charles , *Viaje de un naturalista por la Patagonia* (Marymar)
Davies, Howell, *De Gales a la Patagonia* (Argentina Austral)
D´ Orbigny, Alcides, *Viaje a la América meridional* (Futuro)
Ebelot, Alfredo, *Relatos de la frontera* (Solar)
Falkner, Thomas, *Descripción de la Patagonia y de las partes contiguas*, (Hachette)
Ferns, H. S., *Gran Bretaña y la Argentina en el siglo XIX* (Solar)
García Enciso, Isaías José, *La gesta de Patagones* (Eudeba)
Goldsmith-Carter, George, *Veleros de todo el mundo* (Bruguera)
Goodall, Rae N. Prosser de, *Tierra del Fuego* (Shanamaüm)
Hosne, Roberto, *"Historias del Río de la Plata", "Los Andes, Historias de Héroes, pioneros y transgresores"* (Planeta), *"Patagonia, Leyenda y realidad"* (Eudeba)
Hourcade, Luis, *Los primeros colonos en las islas Malvinas* (Argentina Austral)
Hudson, Guillermo E., *Días de ocio en la Patagonia* (Marymar)
Lewin, Boleslao, *Popper: un conquistador patagónico* (Candelabro)
Llaras Samitier, Manuel, *Rumbo a la Patagonia* (Plus Ultra)
Madsen, Andreas, *La Patagonia vieja* (Galerna)
Martínez, José Luis, *Pasajeros de Indias* (Alianza)
Moreno, Eduardo, *Reminiscencias de Francisco P. Moreno* (Eudeba)
Moreno, Francisco P., *"Viaje a la Patagonia austral"* (Solar/Hachette)
Musters, George Ch., *Vida entre los patagones* (Solar/Hachette)

Onelli, Clemente, *Trepando los Andes* (Marymar)
Parish, Woodbine, *Buenos Aires y las Provincias Unidas del Río de La Plata* (Hachette)
Payró, Roberto J., *La Australia argentina* (Eudeba)
Pigafetta, Antonio, *Primer viaje en torno del globo* (Espasa)
Saint-Exupéry, Antoine de, *Vuelo nocturno* (Hyspamérica)
Sarmiento de Gamboa, P., *Viajes al Estrecho de Magallanes* (Emecé)
Silberstein, Enrique, *Piratas, Filibusteros, Corsarios y Bucaneros,* (Carlos Pérez Editor)
Walther, J.C., *La conquista del desierto* (Eudeba)
Willis, Bailey, *"El norte de la Patagonia","Historia de la Comisión de Estudios hidrológicos del Ministerio de Obras Públicas"*
Ygobone, Aquiles D., *Viajeros científicos de la Patagonia,* Galerna, y *Francisco P. Moreno* (Plus Ultra)
Zeballos, Estanislao, *Viaje al país de los araucanos* (Solar)
Zweig, Stefan, *Magallanes* (Buenos Aires)

PHOTOGRAPHS

Archivo General de la Nación
Continente (Editorial Viscontea)
Baires Magazine
Swing Editora
Secretaría de Turismo de la Nación